"Even given the promises of queer theory, it is wonderful that an author returns to generative fields of feminism, sexual difference, psychoanalysis, and feminine desire. The book's ideas are vibrant, unexpected, outside traditional feminist disputations, but without giving up sexuality, desire or a feminist project. Interrogating feminine desire is imperative, leaving Woman to prescriptive Jungian avatars is too dangerous in these times where culture commodifies identities and desire with such startling speed and normative results."

Kareen Malone, Professor Emerita of Psychology, University of West Georgia, USA and program co-chair of the Atlanta Psychoanalytic Society

"Dr. Morris provides an innovative and much-needed intervention into the relation of psychoanalysis to contemporary thought on gender and sexuality. In this nuanced and carefully thought exploration of women as monstrous in this late-stage capitalist society, she extends, explicates, and entangles the psychoanalysis of Lacan with extensions of his work in interlocutors such as Kristeva and Ettinger. Morris opens new avenues for us to think about the way we see women as monstrous across different sociohistorical contexts. Developing the work of immanent theorists such as Deleuze and Guattari, as well as Braidotti, she engages the possibility that social anxiety in response to the female as inherently aberrant may indicate 'an almost ungovernable excess between the assumed norm and the identified other'. In this rich reading of gender, sexuality, culture, and abjection, Morris delves into horror films, literature, feminist psychology, psychoanalysis, and cultural studies. This incisive and insightful book is well worth the journey."

Kathleen Skott-Myhre, Associate Professor of Psychology, University of West Georgia, USA

Sexual Difference, Abjection and Liminal Spaces

This book uses an interdisciplinary approach to explore the ways in which sexual difference can be understood as an encounter with otherness through the abjected, investigating social discourses and unconscious anxieties around "monstrous" women throughout history and how they may challenge these characterizations.

The author expands on Barbara Creed's notion of the monstrous-feminine to give a specifically Lacanian analysis of different types of feminine monsters, such as Mary Toft, Andrea Yates, Lillith, and Medusa. Drawing on Lacan's theory of "sexuation," the book interrogates characterizations of pregnant women during the Enlightenment, women who commit filicide, mothers in the psychoanalytic clinic, and women with borderline personality disorder. Chapters explore how encounters with a feminine subject in the Lacanian sense can manifest in misogynistic practices aimed at women, as well as how a Deleuzian notion of becoming-other may pose a challenge to their interpretation in a phallocentric meaning-making system. Creatively engaging the work of both Jacques Lacan and Gilles Deleuze, the text goes beyond simply identifying misogynistic practices by probing the relational, unconscious dynamics between hegemonic groups and those designated as "other."

Approaching the concept of the borderline from a critical and transdisciplinary perspective, this text will appeal to postgraduate students and researchers from Lacanian psychoanalysis, gender studies, cultural studies, and critical psychology.

Bethany Morris is Assistant Professor of Psychology at Point Park University. She has her PhD from the University of West Georgia, USA and her research interests include Lacanian psychoanalysis, discourse analysis, and gender and sexuality.

Lines of the Symbolic Series in Psychoanalysis
Series Editor:
Ian Parker, Manchester Psychoanalytic Matrix

Psychoanalytic clinical and theoretical work is always embedded in specific linguistic and cultural contexts and carries their traces, traces which this series attends to in its focus on multiple contradictory and antagonistic "lines of the Symbolic." This series takes its cue from Lacan's psychoanalytic work on three registers of human experience, the Symbolic, the Imaginary and the Real, and employs this distinctive understanding of culture, communication, and embodiment to link with other traditions of cultural, clinical, and theoretical practice beyond the Lacanian symbolic universe. *Lines of the Symbolic Series in Psychoanalysis* provides a reflexive reworking of theoretical and practical issues, translating psychoanalytic writing from different contexts, grounding that work in the specific histories and politics that provide the conditions of possibility for its descriptions and interventions to function. The series makes connections between different cultural and disciplinary sites in which psychoanalysis operates, questioning the idea that there could be one single correct reading and application of Lacan. Its authors trace their own path, their own line through the Symbolic, situating psychoanalysis in relation to debates which intersect with Lacanian work, explicating it, extending it, and challenging it.

From the Conscious Interior to an Exterior Unconscious
Lacan, Discourse Analysis, and Social Psychology
David Pavón Cuéllar

The Constitution of the Psychoanalytic Clinic
A History of its Structure and Power
Christian Dunker

Pink Herrings
Fantasy, Object Choice, and Sexuation
Damien W. Riggs

Sexual Difference, Abjection and Liminal Spaces
A Psychoanalytic Approach to the Abhorrence of the Feminine
Bethany Morris

Sexual Difference, Abjection and Liminal Spaces

A Psychoanalytic Approach to the Abhorrence of the Feminine

Bethany Morris

LONDON AND NEW YORK

First published 2020
by Routledge
2 Park Square, Milton Park, Abingdon, Oxon OX14 4RN

and by Routledge
52 Vanderbilt Avenue, New York, NY 10017

Routledge is an imprint of the Taylor & Francis Group, an informa business

© 2020 Bethany Morris

The right of Bethany Morris to be identified as author of this work has been asserted by her in accordance with sections 77 and 78 of the Copyright, Designs and Patents Act 1988.

All rights reserved. No part of this book may be reprinted or reproduced or utilized in any form or by any electronic, mechanical, or other means, now known or hereafter invented, including photocopying and recording, or in any information storage or retrieval system, without permission in writing from the publishers.

Trademark notice: Product or corporate names may be trademarks or registered trademarks, and are used only for identification and explanation without intent to infringe.

British Library Cataloguing-in-Publication Data
A catalogue record for this book is available from the British Library

Library of Congress Cataloging-in-Publication Data
A catalog record has been requested for this book

ISBN: 978-0-367-17334-0 (hbk)
ISBN: 978-0-367-17339-5 (pbk)
ISBN: 978-0-429-05626-0 (ebk)

Typeset in Times
by Integra Software Services Pvt. Ltd.

For Ruth and Kevin, for your continued love and support.

Contents

About the author x
Author's note xi
Series preface xii
Acknowledgements xiv

1 Introduction 1

2 Sexuation and becoming-woman 10

3 Sexual difference in mythology 32

4 Sexual difference and the medical gaze 50

5 Psychoanalysis and the mother-monster 65

6 Fairytales and femme fatales 89

7 The borderline, jouissance, and capitalist enjoyment 111

8 The monster is in the meme: Transgender people and sexual difference 124

Index 136

About the author

Bethany Morris is Assistant Professor of Psychology at Point Park University in Pittsburgh. She has her PhD from the University of West Georgia in Psychology: Consciousness and Society. She is originally from Prince Edward Island, Canada. Her research interests are interdisciplinary with an appreciation for psychoanalysis, discourse analysis, film, and feminist theory.

Author's note

Lacanian psychoanalysts and scholars differ in the ways in which they present Lacanian terminology. For this reason, the Lacanian terms *Symbolic*, *Real*, and *Imaginary* are all capitalized to denote their reference. Similarly, when the word *Other* is capitalized, it refers to the Lacanian Other, as opposed to an additional person. Furthermore, *he* is used to demarcate the masculine position, as is *she* to demarcate the feminine position, though this does not mean I am necessarily referring to biologically sexed males or females, as explicated in this book. Finally, I also use the capitalized *Woman* to refer to the Lacanian Woman, that is, the woman who does not exist, whereas woman simply refers to the gendered identity of woman.

Series preface

Sexual difference, at the core, the real of this book, is refracted through the historically constituted symbolic stuff that makes of us human beings, of whatever gender, speaking beings. The symbolic production and reproduction of femininity, its forms of grotesque abjection and glimmering resistance, is then experienced in the multitude of contradictory imaginary attempts to grasp and communicate what it is to be a sexed subject to others, and to ourselves. The wide-ranging compass of this book shows us so well how those imaginary attempts to make sense of sexual difference operate in such a way as to totalize and fix in place women, to do that in such a way as to render the feminine into something abhorrent. This conceptual journey requires us to think again about what that "real" of sexual difference is, and to configure it in Lacanian psychoanalytic terms rather than in the essentialist and universalizing imaginary terms employed by so much psychiatric and psychological popular discourse. Only in that way can we really appreciate how important the lines of the symbolic are in tracing and conditioning what women are understood to be, insisting on the marginalizing and disparaging of women while also, paradoxically, idealizing her.

And, in a necessary and carefully handled explication of numerous vantage points on this question that give such rich depth to psychoanalysis, Bethany Morris also shows us why a critically reflexive take on Lacan's contribution needs to also situate psychoanalysis as such in the lines of the symbolic. Lacanian psychoanalysis is a historically conditioned theoretical practice, and the diverse, multiple standpoints on what "femininity" is are inexplicable without an appreciation of the diverse multiple standpoints on what Lacanian psychoanalysis itself is. To be truly Lacanian is to map how psychoanalytic concepts—and here it is sexual difference that is in question—operate in a conceptual field that ranges from Deleuze and Guattari to Julia Kristeva and Bracha Ettinger. As each of these figures, and more, help us to read the ways we have been constituted as speaking beings, they embed us historically, and open up psychoanalysis to history and mythology. Then it is possible to really grasp, while simultaneously taking a critical distance from, potent toxic images of abjection and the role of liminal spaces in and around horror films and dominant ideological representations of trans. This book is an analysis and crafted meditation on sexual difference that is designed to make a difference.

Psychoanalytic clinical and theoretical work circulates through multiple intersecting antagonistic symbolic universes. This series opens connections between different cultural sites in which Lacanian work has developed in distinctive ways, in forms of work that question the idea that there could be single correct reading and application. The *Lines of the Symbolic Series in Psychoanalysis* series provides a reflexive reworking of psychoanalysis that transmits Lacanian writing from around the world, steering a course between the temptations of a metalanguage and imaginary reduction, between the claim to provide a god's eye view of psychoanalysis, and the idea that psychoanalysis must everywhere be the same. And the elaboration of psychoanalysis in the symbolic here grounds its theory and practice in the history and politics of the work in a variety of interventions that touch the real.

Ian Parker
Manchester Psychoanalytic Matrix

Acknowledgements

I was able to write this book because I had the fortunate opportunity to immerse myself in the truly unique Psychology department at the University of West Georgia. There I found the true spirit of academia—curiosity, consideration, and intellectual love affairs with foundational thinkers. Thank you to Hans and Kathy who pushed me to get out of my intellectual comfort zone and ushered me into the academic world. To John, whose depth of knowledge and kindness made the experience both challenging and exciting. To Kareen, I am grateful for the time and consideration you have granted me and all that I have learned from you. Finally, to Neill, for helping me to realize not only what I want to do with my life, but how to do it compassionately, and ultimately, with a sense of humor.

I want to thank Ian Parker for providing me the opportunity to contribute to his series. Even as I write this, it feels a touch surreal. Ian Parker's books were my introduction to both Psychoanalytic theory and Critical Psychology. I can only describe this opportunity as likely being akin to going on tour with your favorite rock star.

I am eternally grateful for my colleagues, Chase and Sebastienne. Without your kindness, wit, and patience, I would have been lost, literally and existentially.

Thank you to my sweet family. To the Aronsons, for your continued support and wisdom. To my parents, who have always encouraged me to pursue my passions, and for trusting me to choose wisely, even though I did not always. If my foray into psychoanalysis has taught me anything, it is your fault I am the way I am, and I am exceptionally grateful for that. Finally, to Alexander, who reminds me daily of what it means to pursue a life of love, warmth, and Lacan. I look forward to continuing to learn with and from you.

Chapter 1

Introduction

In 1955, Lacan (2006) made a proclamation that psychoanalysis and its practitioners needed to return to Freud, claiming that Freud's antecedents were betraying the radical principles of the field. Lacan was witnessing the advent of ego psychology and the eclipsing of the unconscious by the ego as the site of experience. In doing so, Freud's insights were at risk of being lost to a "science" of the reified ego. I do not say "science" out of derision, but rather to demarcate the tension between psychoanalysis and psychological sciences, as well to note the shift in psychoanalysis toward mainstream practices that it originally sought to critique. This book comes out of a similar concern. That is, a concern about the reification of the ego at the expense of the unconscious, both our own and others. The history of harmful and horrific practices against women has concerned me since learning about Sarah Baartman, "The Hottentot Venus," in an undergraduate 18th century literature class, in which behaviors were justified because the person who was subjected to them was deemed less than human. The contemporary moment has its own horrors with the unrelenting #MeToo stories, the wave of attempts to overturn or counter *Roe v. Wade* in the United States, and attacks on women's safety around the world.

My concern, and what I hope to bring to the discussion about our current climate of social issues, is an obfuscation of sexual difference in the discourse about the tension between the sexes. Sexual difference has been the site of a longstanding debate between American and French Feminism, and though both sides offer important tools for thinking about the status of women in the 21st century, the concerns of French feminism, as born out of psychoanalysis, offer sharp critiques of the American sect as well as provide nuanced ways to consider sexual difference as a site of potential for combating oppression. Sexual difference, especially in the Lacanian tradition, takes seriously the relationship with the Other, as in the one to which we attempt to account for in our own unconscious. In doing so, it retains the dichotomy of two sexes, but challenges the status quo binary system predicated on biological differences and allows for a consideration of anxiety in the face of difference. The reason this is important is because it runs contrary to as to those discourses that focus on hatred, power, and conscious intention on the part of the perpetrator of discrimination, prejudice, or violence. While compassion for such individuals may, upon first glance, seem unwarranted, the Lacanian tradition allows for a way of considering the ways in which we all confront anxiety in the face of difference. It is this anxiety, the anxiety of Man, the patriarchy, or the oppressor, that I want to consider, and emphasize by considering it as in response to the horror of sexual difference.

By horror, I mean that distinct, inconsolable affect that dances around an encounter without ever quite resting comfortably on an appropriate signifier. Horror tends to have negative connotations in contemporary Western society, with associations to blood and gore, supernatural creatures, and threats to one's life. While these associations are dominant, my intention in using the word *horror* in relation to sexual difference is to consider the subjective state of inarticulable anxiety elicited in the confrontation with an other *whose very presence undermines one's own*. This type of horror goes beyond maimed body parts and instead threatens one's conceptualization of one's humanity or subjectivity. By coming to terms with this idea, those beliefs, practices, and interventions aimed at regulating the behavior and practices of the other can be understood as an attempt to eradicate this horror. To state it another way, practices which attempt to efface manifestations of sexual difference are not simply acts of misogyny or examples of patriarchal oppression, but rather should be understood as a complicated nexus of anxiety, resistance, liberation, and disruption.

In order to guide my analysis of these encounters, I utilize a hybrid theoretical analysis, relying heavily on the works of and contributors to the psychoanalytic theories of Jacques Lacan and Julia Kristeva, as well as Gilles Deleuze and Felix Guattari. Jacques Lacan offers a theory of the modern Western subject, as constituted by and through language, and began to articulate the problem of sexual difference as posited by Freud's now-infamous question, "What do women want?" Specifically, it is Lacan's consideration of the feminine subject and feminine jouissance as that which cannot be spoken about, and that which harkens to a time prior to an individualized subject that I identify as the foundation of sexual difference. More specifically, it is Julia Kristeva's take on the abject and abjection as being intimately tied to sexual difference that I utilize to uncover the ways in which approaches to either explicate or efface the notion of sexual difference inevitably create a moral exclusion or outcast in the form of the monstrous-feminine.

Gilles Deleuze and Felix Guattari will guide my analysis of this monstrous-feminine in considering the ways in which these encounters could be understood as having latent potential in considering subjectivity and its deconstruction in the contemporary moment. Specifically, I argue that their concept "becoming-woman" (Deleuze and Guattari, 1980), which they argue is the first stage of challenging the rigid conditions of the human being, relies on Lacan's notion of Woman that is, the woman under erasure. It is not my intention to suggest that Deleuze and Guattari take up Lacanian analysis where Lacan was unable to go, as their projects diverged in such ways that such a statement would do none of these theorists justice. Rather, in this book, I speculate about how those encounters with instantiations of sexual difference can first be accounted for through a Lacanian understanding of sexuation and jouissance, and then demonstrate how they may have had an effect on the subject in such a way that his assumptions about the Other, and thus relations to, may have been altered. This is not to assume an understanding of the subjects in question, nor would this be akin to a psychoanalysis of their behavior. Rather, I would like to think about the subjects discussed as both constituted, and unable to be adequately constituted, by different dominant discourses, with the assumptions that these subjects exist in a map, as opposed to some sort of teleological progression of discourses.

Horror and sexual difference

The research on gender and horror, monsters or monstrosity is vast. Horror films in particular have received a great deal of consideration for both their perpetuation of sexist and violent attitudes toward women, as well as for their potential to challenge and subvert hegemonic gender discourses. Similarly, many works of fiction that have been identified as horror, gothic, or thriller have been investigated through the lenses of gender theory, as well as abjection. Psychoanalyst Julia Kristeva (1982) uses literature from Kafka, Artaud, and Dostoevsky, among others, as a means to discuss and exemplify her notion of the abject, which will be elaborated on shortly. Most of the scholarly literature on sexual difference and horror is in regard to gender roles and issues pertaining to violence and aggression toward women. For this reason, I will engage with literature that provides opportunities to discuss sexual difference beyond the level of symbolic distinctions, and grapples with those distinctions that pertain to epistemological differences within sexuation as mentioned previously. For these reasons, I will stick to a discussion of two specific texts here: Carol Clover's *Men, women and chain saws: Gender in the modern horror film* and Barbara Creed's *The monstrous-feminine: Film, feminism and psychoanalysis*.

The final girl

Carol Clover's (1992) book *Men, women and chainsaws: Gender in the modern horror film* is one of the seminal texts on gender and horror films. She focuses on American horror films from the 1970s and 1980s in which the issue of gender seems to be pertinent, specifically in slasher films, occult or possession films, and rape-revenge films. Clover's work seems to respond to the question: Who watches horror films? as well as the assumption that the audience is male, with questions about identification, especially in those films that include a "final girl." The final girl is the female protagonist in a horror film who, after the monster or murderer has slaughtered all or the majority of the characters, is left to confront and destroy the monster. Clover claims that horror movie audiences, who have been typically male, have been thought to identify with the monster or serial killer and in doing so are able to vicariously commit acts of violence against women that they would be punished for in real life. The male spectator then is one who has unconscious fantasies of murder or rape and sublimates it by watching depictions of such acts as entertainment. Such an explanation reinforces assumptions about men as inherently aggressive and the aggressor. This is similar to Laura Mulvey's (1992) consideration of the sadistic-voyeuristic male gaze, in which she argues that such films are designed with a male gaze in mind. Specifically, she makes the case that voyeurism is inherently pleasurable, and that that pleasure lies in the gaze's ability to ascertain guilt, assert control, and be the arbiter of punishment or forgiveness for the guilty person.

Clover's point is not to contradict Mulvey's conception of the male gaze, nor detract from its influence. Rather, she seeks to make an addendum, suggesting that identification is perhaps more equivocal than Mulvey posited. Clover follows Freud's argument about the enduring power of certain stories, claiming that they allow for a safe engagement with repressed desires and fears, as well as a means for re-enactment. While this does not initially sound different from Mulvey's argument, its implications stretch further. Clover suggests that the horror movie is structured in such a way that this assumed male audience likely also identifies with the final girl. She argues that the spectator is both the wolf and the young girl in Little Red Riding Hood, just as we are both attacker and victim in the horror film, because the horror derives from having an apprehension of both sides. Furthermore, the final girl collapses the victim and hero dichotomy, traditionally a female and male dichotomy, and she is at once both. The spectator similarly must struggle with impotence and virility in the hopes of vanquishing the monster, whether it be a man in a mask with a chainsaw or an amorphous consuming blob.

The monstrous-feminine

While Clover's work is both creative and impressive, her work deals largely with gender identifications. In contrast, Barbara Creed (1999) explicitly takes on a psychoanalytic investigation about the role of castration in horror films, and thus attempting to account for the unconscious. She challenges traditional assumptions about feminine monsters, namely that, according to Freudian theory, the woman evokes terror or horror because she is assumed to be castrated. This horror is akin to the horror that the male child experiences during his Oedipal development, in which he realizes that women, as exemplified by his mother, are lacking the phallus, and that it must have been taken from her. Thus, he develops castration anxiety, which motivates his sublimation into a number of behaviors, not to mention psychosexual theories. Stephen Neale (1980) in his book *Genre* argues that the male monster in horror films functions to fill the lack, that is, to disavow their castration, defending against the all-consuming anxiety that it provokes. He argues further, that, most monsters are male because they take woman as the object of their desire, not with a heteronormative assumption but rather in relation to lack and the phallus. In contrast, Susan Lurie (1981) argues that man fears woman not because she is castrated, but rather because she is not castrated and marked in the way that he would be if were to be castrated. Rather than being horrified at her lack, man instead fears that she will castrate him.

Barbara Creed, while appreciating Lurie's contradiction to Neale's argument, is not satisfied with her approach as it assumes, like Neale, that the monster is inherently male. Creed, on the other hand, is interested in those monsters which are feminine. She argues that there are monsters in horror films which are distinctly feminine, and not simply female monsters in the male role. Rather, she seeks to ascertain precisely what monstrous-femininity entails and, relying on Kristeva's psychoanalytic theories, why it is so frightening. Following Williams (1984) piece explicating the similarities between monsters and women, suggesting that the woman spectator has an affinity with the monster as the site of threatening sexuality, Creed seeks to delve deeper into this affinity. She makes an argument that the monstrous-feminine is usually expressed in relation to her reproductive and mothering capacities, which she identifies as the monstrous womb, the witch, the vampire, and the possessed woman. To defend her assertion, she uses Kristeva's (1982) work on abjection, which I will elaborate on later, and the conflicting desires elicited by the maternal body.

Similar to Clover, however, Creed also remains within film in order to discuss the monstrous-feminine. Janisse (2012) goes one step further in her autobiographical cartography of women in horror film, in which she weaves personal narrative through her *House of psychotic women*. Her book is one of the largest compilations of representations of the monstrous-feminine in horror films and she illuminates these films with vivid descriptions and intense analysis. However, similar to Clover and Creed, that analysis remains strictly within the realm of film analysis. This is not a critique, but rather a consideration as to where I would like to situate this book: a convergence of the humanities, the social sciences, psychoanalytic, and feminist theory grounded in sociocultural research. Similar to research using Lacan and Kristeva, the monstrous-feminine, or sexual difference for that matter, has been an endeavor largely investigated by scholars within the humanities, leaving those in the human sciences to consider those matters that they can evaluate empirically. This book attempts to bring some of these considerations developed within the disciplines of Literature, Philosophy, and Film Studies to a consideration of the human subject within a number of contexts, with a conviction that the human subject cannot be compartmentalized by disciplines, and that psychoanalysis offers a rich collection of theories and methodologies through which to think the sociohistorical subject and the question of sexual difference.

Why film?

In a number of the chapters, I weave examples and explanations pertaining to films alongside considerations of archival material. Though I garner much pleasure and many insights from films, I do not pretend to be a film theorist. Many of the observations made about the films in this book may be quite obvious to a dedicated film theorist or connoisseur, or completely inaccurate in some circles. However, it is my intention to understand films as an arena of discourses that become culturally embedded in contemporary society. The result is that films and the various modes of knowledge production about subjectivity intimately become intertwined. Furthermore, though film is often used within the humanities as a legitimate sight of investigation about culture and subjectivity, they have largely been ignored in the social sciences, typically because of the assumption that they are open to interpretation and fail to offer empirical observations. For this book, film then becomes an important hinge through which to communicate the rich theoretical insights produced by psychoanalysis, philosophy, and the humanities with the social sciences, such as psychology and sociology, who claim to take culture and subjectivity as their sights of inquiry. Art and literature has been at the forefront of investigations into the psyche long before the arrival of psychology and sociology, and I believe the social sciences could benefit from a renaissance.

In using film as a means through which to discuss sexual difference and anxiety, it became clear that horror would be my genre of choice. Though I could have just as easily sampled from a number of genres, horror has a complicated home within the discourse of sexual difference. As I will further elaborate on, scholars in psychoanalytic theory and feminist theory have used horror as the vehicle of investigation, such as Laura Mulvey, Carol Glover, and Barbara Creed. Horror also speaks to certain existential anxieties that cannot adequately be symbolized, such as sexual difference, and is elicited in a number of ways that require the suspension of symbolic laws and norms, and demand an encounter the inarticulable. While other genres may attempt to produce a similar encounter, such as fantasy or science fiction, a good horror demonstrates the potential subjective destitution that an encounter with difference can elicit and thus deromanticizes alterity to demonstrate that difference without resolution is intensely distressing. Horror, then, provides a rich tapestry to explore anxiety without an object.

This book will utilize Jacques Lacan's notion of sexuation and sexual difference as a means to elucidate some of these encounters. Chapter 2, "Sexuation and becoming-woman," includes an introductory primer to Lacanian psychoanalysis and Lacan's theory of sexuation, which rests on his claim that there is no sexual relation, meaning that the differences between the sexes cannot be reconciled because they are grounded in different epistemological assumptions. It is then my intention not to contrast, but braid together Lacan's contemporaries', Gilles Deleuze and Felix Guattari, theory of becoming-woman, which emphasizes a consideration of subjectivity as an encounter that is implicitly political. Through an understanding of Lacan's notions of the "Woman" and sexual difference, Deleuze and Guattari's philosophy can be explored further for its implications.

Following this primer chapter, I then make the case that patriarchal societies are organized around a masculine epistemological framework, premised in the prevalence and primacy of the phallus and phallic signifiers; I propose that a confrontation with sexual difference, specifically with femininity in the Lacanian sense, and the impossibility of the sexual relation can produce experiences of horror and what Julia Kristeva referred to as abjection, which elicits both disgust and a preoccupation with the abject. This book will look at what could be called feminine monstrosity. In this sense, monstrosity may not refer to literal monsters, though characters such as Medusa and sirens are discussed, but rather feminine subjects who are treated as if they are monsters, such as pregnant women during the Enlightenment, mothers in the psychoanalytic clinic, women who commit filicide, and women with borderline personality disorder, amongst others.

Chapter 3, "Sexual difference in mythology," begins this investigation with a consideration of the Greek and Christian mythology that has influenced both psychoanalytic and feminist scholarship. Specifically, I will look at the myths of Medusa, the Sphinx, and Oedipus and the sirens in *The Odyssey*, as well as the story of Adam and Eve in the Bible, with special consideration of the inclusion/removal of Lilith from the canonical revisions of the Bible. These stories contain within them questions about sexual difference, specifically what a type of woman may want. The true horror of these tales comes when the male protagonists realize that these women do not want their phallus, or the signifier mistakenly assumed it be the cause of their desire, and they are no longer able to adequately navigate their relation to the Other. The fear is unconsciously linked to a loss of subjectivity.

The next chapter, "Sexual difference and the medical gaze," takes a slight Foucaultian perspective and moves into the Enlightenment era in order to demonstrate the ways in which questions about sexual difference still inform practices even when objectivity is supposedly privileged. By using Foucault's (1973) understanding of the medical gaze, the epistemic knowledge of the time produced about phenomena such as maternal impressions and maternal imagination, constructs its subjects and objects of inquiry. Because of this, the question about the desire of woman finds representation in practices surrounding pregnant women and their imaginations, which can be still observed in the contemporary repertoire about pregnant woman, as evidenced by both film and medical practices regulating and restricting the pregnant body.

Chapter 5, "Psychoanalysis and the mother-monster," turns the analytic gaze back on to psychoanalysis itself, and specifically, the conditions of Freud's famous question, "What does a woman want?" In doing so, I demonstrate how Freud's question allows Lacan to conceive of his theory of sexuation, but more importantly for this work, also contributes in creating a new type of feminine monster, specifically the mother-monster of the unconscious. From here, Lacan's subjective structures can be said to demonstrate how the mother in the unconscious, that is, the unconscious experience of the person in the mother function, revolves around the inability to ascertain the desire of the woman. This becomes realized in a number of ways, such as popular horror films, as well as two particularly high-profile filicide cases during the 1990s in the United States.

Chapter 6, "The femme fatale," expands the term to consider a variety of representations of femininity, death, and power. I suggest that the femme fatale serves as a cautionary tale for both girls and young women about the woman who assumes to possess the phallus and can be found in stories that feature an evil queen. While there are a number of such stories, I explore different instantiations of the Evil Queen in various interpretations of the Snow White story to emphasize the discourses about female development and sexual difference. I follow this developmental trajectory to consider the melancholic feminine, as posited by Julia Kristeva, as a particularly strong referent in popular culture marketed at adolescent women, in which femininity and lifelessness are interrelated. I then turn to the relationship between the femme fatale and the male spectator, considering the implications for the fantasy of the woman who posits the destruction of the man. This fantasy is then reflected in the discourse in online communities, such as Men Going Their Own Way (MGTOWs) and Incels, in which all women resemble a femme fatale.

Chapter 7, "The borderline, jouissance, and capitalist enjoyment," focuses specifically on psychological discourse attempts to render the woman captured within the diagnosis of borderline personality disorder as fearsome. Here, I address biopolitics and sexual difference under neoliberal capitalism. To do this, I refer to the borderline, which I identify as the person, usually woman, within the diagnostic criteria for borderline personality disorder to demonstrate the ways in which neoliberal capitalist discourses have created a new type of feminine monster in their failure to account for the Woman. The borderline, I argue, has become a monster constituted by a failure to operate adequately within neoliberal capitalist discourse as found in psychiatric nomenclature. From a Lacanian perspective, it is demonstrated how the borderline exemplifies the not-all, with one foot imperfectly within the Symbolic and one foot in the Real. This is similar to the other feminine monsters in this book, with the exception that neoliberal capitalist discourses premised on a lack of a lack exacerbate the hysteric subject to the point that she becomes the borderline monster.

The final chapter will consider the ways in which contemporary concerns and debates about transgender people, in particular transwomen in public bathrooms, posit transgender people as a contemporary monster. Similar to the earlier chapters, the anxiety about the presence of transwomen in the bathrooms that correspond to their gender reflect a concern about the status of the phallus in the face of the Other. The increasing prevalence of representations of transgender people in the media, as well as the ongoing violence against them, means that it is vital to consider questions about sexual difference and anxiety, especially in those practices aimed at oppressing or restricting individuals who do not conform to hegemonic norms. A Lacanian interpretation, with a Deleuzian appreciation for an engagement with the political sphere via the unconscious, allows for a rethinking of femininity as threatening, anxiety, or horror in the face of sexual difference, as well as the importance of historical contingencies on the production of knowledge about human subjects. Such considerations also hold the potential to return to questions about how to reconceptualize suffering as a conflict between the desire of the subject and the demands of the Other, something we are all afflicted with.

References

Clover, C. (1992). *Men, women, and chainsaws: Gender in the modern horror film*. Princeton, NJ: Princeton University Press.
Creed, B. (1999). *The monstrous-feminine: Film, feminism and psychoanalysis*. New York: Routledge.
Deleuze, G. and Guattari, F. (1980). *A thousand plateaus: Capitalism and schizophrenia*. Minneapolis, MN: University of Minnesota Press.
Foucault, M. (1973). *The birth of the clinic*. New York: Pantheon Books.
Janisse, K.L. (2012). *House of psychotic women: An autobiographical topography of female neurosis in horror and exploitation films*. Godalming: FAB Press.
Kristeva, J. (1982). *Powers of horror: An essay on abjection*. New York: Columbia University Press.
Lacan, J. (2006). *Ecrits: The complete first edition in English*. New York: W.W. Norton & Co.
Lurie, S. (1981). The construction of the "castrated woman" in psychoanalysis and cinema. *Discourse*, 4(4), 52–74.
Mulvey, L. (1992). Visual pleasure and narrative cinema. In L. Braudy and M. Cohen (Eds.), *Film theory and criticism: An introduction* (833–844). New York: Oxford University Press.
Neale, N. (1980). *Genre*. London: British Film Institute.
Williams, L. (1984). When the woman looks. In M.A. Doane's, P. Mellencamp and L. Williams (Eds.), *Re-vision: Essays in feminist film criticism* (83–99). Frederick: University Publications of America.

Chapter 2

Sexuation and becoming-woman

This book takes an explicitly Lacanian psychoanalysis perspective of subjectivity and sexual difference for a number of reasons. First, Lacanian psychoanalysis, in particular, offers a unique perspective on the human subject as being created and alienated in language, and thus provides an opportunity to work from both structural and poststructural approaches. Lacanian psychoanalysis also assumes that all individuals are neurotically or psychotically structured, and therefore, any notion of mental illness or disorder is considered inherent to the human condition. Such an understanding provides a compelling explanation of a great deal of issues, and in particular, the issue of sexual difference, in a way that is not reduced to causal explanations, but rather one which appreciates the constant struggles and tensions between subjectivity, sexuality, and anxiety. Lastly, Lacan's (1975) incitement to women to say something regarding their experience and the nature of their desire has spawned theoretically rich and creative formulations about the feminine position and its relation to language, art, and madness. It is within this tradition, specifically Kristeva, in which I find the most provocative theorizations in relation to ideas of the monstrous-feminine, as well as the borderline, without deviating too much from the complexity and intricateness of Lacanian psychoanalysis.

For readers less familiar with Lacanian psychoanalysis, it pertains to a specific branch within psychoanalysis proposed by Jacques Lacan. Lacan was a French psychoanalyst in Paris, who was both prominent and controversial during the 1940s–1970s for advocating for a return to Freud as a means for fleshing out his ideas in the face of diverging theorists, such as Melanie Klein or some of the American ego psychologists. According to Lacan, Freud's descendants either deviated too far from Freud or misunderstood him and thus were misguided in their practice. Though he claimed to be a Freudian, Lacan was advancing his own complex and intricate psychoanalytic theory that both appreciated and deviated from Freud's iterations. For example, he took Freud's ideas of the Oedipus complex and neuroses and grounded them in a structural approach, both following and critiquing the work of Sausseure on language. He also developed a structural model of the unconscious Freud discovered, in which there is a Symbolic, Imaginary, and Real (Vanier, 2000).

As I mentioned, Lacan (2006) grounded Freudian theory in language. To do this, he asserted that the unconscious is structured like a language. In saying this, he meant that the unconscious is made up of signifiers, and that one signifier does not have any inherent meaning, but rather points to another signifier. A sentence cannot be understood until the final signifier is in place, and similarly, the signifiers in the unconscious, which make themselves known through dreams, slips of the tongue, and other Freudian techniques, only have meaning in relation to the signifying chain in which they are embedded. Signifiers make up the unconscious because it is through language in which we come into being as an individual, and how we come to organize our desire (Lacan, 2006). Lacan suggested that this occurs during the mirror stage, which is the time that the infant becomes subjectivized by learning to associate the mirror image to the coalescence of drives that constituted the experiencing organism (the baby) prior to that moment. Lacan suggests that prior to about six months of age, the infant does not experience herself as a distinct subject, but rather a series of drives and partial objects, such as a mouth, breast, etc., in which the primary caregiver is indiscriminately attached. It is when the primary caregiver points to the infant in the mirror and speaks the infant's name, or reiterates the separateness of the infant from the caregiver through speaking the infant's name, that she begins to formulate a conception of the self as a separate entity.

The Lacanian subject

The notion of the subject undergoes numerous revisions and considerations throughout Lacan's own career, not to mention those who have taken up his work since. For our purposes, there are two points that are important to note. First, it is not the subject of standard Western thought. The Lacanian subject is not the Cartesian subject in which conscious thought dictates subjective development. As Fink (1996) argues, the conscious thinking subject is the ego as understood within Ego Psychology. For Lacan, the ego is an amalgamation of ideal images, which a child learns to identify with. These identifications come from the Other and can take the form of "good girl" or more importantly, as an "I," a unified individual, separate from the Other. For Lacan, these identifications are imaginary, not in a make-believe sense, but in that they are a constellation of images or associations based on interpretations of what the Other wants (Fink, 1996). The Lacanian subject, then, is the subject of the unconscious, and more specifically, the speaking subject of the unconscious. It is important to note that the Lacanian subject is also known as the barred or split subject, which emphasizes the contradictory nature of the subject because she has been cut off from the cause of her desire, and must contend with her competing and contradictory urges.

It is important to note here that the Lacanian subject is always the subject of desire and therefore, reducing it to historical contingencies misses the radicality of Lacanian thought. Joan Copjec (1994) has perhaps been the most vocal in this argument against historicity, which she identifies as "the reduction of a society to its indwelling network of relations of power and knowledge" (p. 14). Her argument is that Lacanian psychoanalysis understands that the appearance of things, whether it be power dynamics or structural institutions, do not supplant being. That subject's being and the person as represented in the egoic ideals are not one and the same, and it is this disjunctive relationship that is the ground of desire. Historicist approaches, she argues, mistakes the subject of desire (being) and the appearance of the person as historically constituted (egoic ideals) as one and the same. I am not suggesting that historicist approaches are not valuable or have not contributed greatly to the understanding of marginalized and oppressed peoples. However, I am curious about the effects if we follow Copjec, and Lacan, and take desire seriously, all the while understanding that desire itself is inarticulable, and that the modern subject is best understood as the subject that is constantly effaced or eclipsed by its egoic manifestations or presentations.

The Symbolic, the Real, and the Imaginary

In order to have a better grasp of the Lacanian subject, an overview of the structures of his unconscious is essential. As previously mentioned, the Imaginary pertains to images, which become the first unconscious material. While this book will rely largely on references to the Symbolic and the Real, a brief consideration of the Imaginary is useful here. The Imaginary emerges prior to the Symbolic as the individual comes to identify with images before she learns language. Vanier (2000) explains that the notion of the Imaginary undergoes the most development in Lacan's (2006) consideration of the mirror stage. As previously mentioned, the mirror stage occurs around six months at age, at which time the child comes to see herself as a separate entity from her primary caregiver. This occurs when the infant comes to associate her name, or monikers such as "good girl," "pretty girl," or "smart girl," with the image in the mirror. For Lacan, an identification occurs at this stage that elicits a transformation in the subject, in which she comes to assume an image, or what he referred to as "an imago" (p. 77). The third party, whether it be a primary caregiver or another who imbues that imago with adjectives, helps to cement this image to the subject, allowing for a gestalt experience of herself, or a unity of her body along with a sense of mastery of it (Vanier, 2000). The ego develops from this sense of unity. What is important to note here is that Lacan makes a distinction between the ego, the imaginary agency or mastery, and the subject. For Lacan, the subject is the subject of language, which will be discussed further in relation to the Symbolic. The ego and the assumed agency of the ego, because it is premised in an image that never quite corresponds to a real, is an identification that alienates the subject, and allows for the development of an alter ego in tandem (Vanier, 2000). The subject is essentially the alienated and conflicted mover beneath the ego, which must contend with his own desires and the demands made upon him.

While the Imaginary functions via images, the Symbolic, another Lacanian unconscious register, is the realm in which signifiers circulate, and thereby, making it the place in which speaking beings reside. According to Lacan, individuals are born into a language that is not their own, meaning that they learn from their primary caregiver. They come to use this language as their own, but because it was not innate, they enter it alienated, as something belonging to the other. As Vanier notes, for Lacan, there ceases to be a subject without the Other. This is important because these inherited signifiers are phallic, meaning that they are the something offered up, such as words and gestures, to the Other as the cause of their desire, understood as akin to the phallus in the sexual relationship. For example, in regard to the example of the infant being cut off from the breast or cause of her desire, the infant will typically cry or emit some form of symbolic gesture that the caregiver responds to. As time goes on, the infant learns different expressions and gestures to communicate to the Other. Therefore, it is a bit simplistic to understand the Lacanian Symbolic as only pertaining to language. It is the range of meaningful acts that consider the desire of the Other and attempt to elicit it. However, and this is crucial to the current investigation, the phallic signifier should always be considered as inherently lacking. This means that it never will be what the other desires, and therefore, individuals will keep trying to offer something else. For Lacan, this is what makes societies function and progress. Scientific and technological advances, not to mention commodities, are all done with the unconscious intention of filling the unconscious lack, but because the lack cannot be filled, humans continue to create, innovate, and, most importantly for the psychoanalyst, speak.

It is within the Symbolic in which sexual difference and gender politics are traditionally considered. Theories about gender performativity and sexual identity (Butler, 1990) are particularly popular in the contemporary feminist discourse, specifically regarding what women are capable of, or what is included in this instantiation of "Woman." While these discussions are not without their own merit, from a Lacanian perspective, such articulations are still considered phallic. That is, the identification of certain traits, or ways of beings that designate a gender, or a lack thereof, are constituted in relation to a signifier that is either present or absent and articulated via language, thereby making it phallic.

If the Symbolic is the realm of signifiers, the Real is the absence of such, making it difficult to adequately explain. Lacan also reformulated his understanding of the Real throughout his career, further complicating attempts to provide one concise definition of this register (Fink, 1996). However, for my purposes here, it will suffice to say that if the child enters the Symbolic via castration from the Other and thus becomes differentiated as a subject, the Real is the undifferentiated drives that make up the organism prior to becoming subjectivized and lays just beyond meaning for the subject. Because the Real cannot be reduced to meaning, making it impossible to represent in the Symbolic, and likewise does not lend itself to imaginary representations in the Imaginary, it is experienced as something that intrudes the subject. Soler (2014) explains that the Real for Lacan transitions from being something that exists at the limits of the Symbolic to that which undergirds the Symbolic, rupturing through via symptoms and jouissance. Furthermore, it is the Real which is at stake in the nature of sexual difference, which will be discussed further in the section on sexuation.

Jouissance and the object a

Another of Lacan's major contributions to psychoanalytic theory and sexual difference is his notion of jouissance. In his early seminars, jouissance is proposed in relation to the master and slave dialectic as proposed by Hegel and refers to what the other supposedly enjoys (Lacan, 2006). In this articulation, it is the mistaken assumption that the other has that mysterious thing that allows him or her to perfectly enjoy life, and that it is attainable, once it is ascertained what "it" is. However, it is in relation to Lacan's theorizations about jouissance as in relation to the Real and the object a in which jouissance can really be understood for its effect on the subject.

It is essential to know that jouissance, like most of Lacanian theory, retroactively originates in infancy and is always in relation to the Other. As explained earlier, the subject speaks, using the language inherited from the Other. The Other is the source of all of the infant's satisfactions and so language functions as a way to keep the Other engaged. As also mentioned earlier, sometimes that satisfaction becomes too much, such is the case with the baby nursing to the point that she is overfed and uncomfortable. Without this intervention, the infant is unable to become a subject unto herself and remains at the whim of the jouissance of the Other. Lacan explains that this intervention is the Name of the Father, which has the thing that the Other must want, or else the Other would be completely gratified by the infant. In keeping with the Freudian Oedipus complex, this "thing" is the phallus, but Lacan emphasizes that the phallus is a signifier. It is interpreted as that which the Other is lacking and what the infant has to assume a relation to, either through having the phallus or not. Levy-Stokes (2001) explains that the subject must forgo being the sole enjoyment of her caregiver, or complete jouissance, in order to become a speaking being. Fink (1996) explains that the assumption that the Other enjoys complete jouissance through the phallus is a fantasy. This fantasy puts the subject in the position to keep speaking, making knowledge the product of a deficiency in jouissance (Fink, 2002). This is why jouissance should be understood as inherently tied to both sexuality and death because, while pleasurable, complete jouissance is annihilation of the subject. This is also why, following Fink (1996), the Lacanian subject should be thought of as the subject not in language, but rather the subject caught between language and jouissance.

Object a, or petite object a, is another original Lacanian term that has undergone significant theorizations by Lacan himself, as well as other scholars and psychoanalysts. For the sake of consistency, I will rely here on Fink's (1996) condensed translation, as well as Mark's (2001) summary. Object a is intimately related to both the Real and jouissance, specifically through the fundamental fantasy surrounding what was lost in surrendering complete jouissance to language. Mark makes note that it is important to distinguish between an object of desire and an object that causes desire. Object a should be understood as the latter, meaning that it is believed to be the thing that the other has which elicits desire. However, this can never be adequately apprehended because it can never be perfectly encapsulated through symbolization. This resistance to meaning is what ties it to the Real, and therefore, the missing piece to complete jouissance. Because this object a is premised in fantasy, its manifestation is malleable, and the subject is able to keep finding/missing it in a variety of interactions. Lacan (2006) asserts that desire is metonymical, and therefore, this object a, by setting in motion desire, is repeatedly displaced, and misapprehended. Jouissance, in conjunction with object a, constitute phallic jouissance (Fink, 1996). Later in his career, he began to consider what it meant for jouissance to be without an object a, and therefore, without desire as a defense. Jouissance without phallic intervention became understood as feminine jouissance.

Lacanian sexuation and epistemology

Through an understanding of feminine jouissance, Lacanian sexual difference can come to be understood as radically different from contemporary conceptualizations of gender identity or sexuality. Lacan uses the term "sexuation" and it should be understood as a reformulation of the Freudian distinction of the sexes in relation to the primacy of the phallus (Stevens, 2012). Sexuation should be understood as a tripartite position, with the first level of sexual difference occurring as an unconscious identification with masculinity or femininity. This does not necessarily correspond to a biological sex, but rather as a speaking subject who either believes himself or herself to have the phallus versus occupies the position of being the phallus. The second position of sexuation occurs in relation to jouissance, or how one enjoys, either exclusively through phallic means, or via the not-all of the phallus. Finally, the third position is in relation to how one understands his or her enjoyment in relation to the Other, specifically how one understands the Other's enjoyment (Stevens, 2012). The implications of this formulation of sexuation is that sexuality is not simply an identification or preference for a certain type of sexual relationship, but is rather an epistemological position with its own inherent logic (Ragland-Sullivan, 2004). This is why Lacan maintained that there was no sexual relation. There is no resolving the aporias of the sexes (Soler, 2003).

The primary identification, for Lacan, is a choice between identifying as a man or as a woman. As mentioned earlier, this is not a choice in regard to biological sex, but rather as an unconscious positional choice in the order of discourse (Stevens, 2012). As Soler (2003) points out, if biological sex corresponded to one's legal sexed status, it clearly does not organize desire or the drives accordingly, given the existence and prevalence of perversions. Lacan maintains that it is the phallus that orients sexuality, providing a very limited amount of representations, and is ultimately based on how the child identifies with the signifier, and the Name of the Father, as communicated via the unconscious desire of the mother (Ragland-Sullivan, 2004). As mentioned earlier, the Name of the Father is what effects castration and allows the child to become a subject, while surrendering a part of his own jouissance.

The second distinguishing factor in Lacan's understanding of sexuation is in relation to jouissance, or how one enjoys. As mentioned earlier, while all subjects experience phallic jouissance in relation to their own object a, some subjects are structurally open to an Other jouissance. Ragland-Sullivan (2004) summarizes the issue aptly, stating,

> Lacking a universalizing signifier—The "Woman"—that would point to some essence of Woman, human beings who do not identify with having a penis, rather, with the Real which inserts a lack in the Symbolic. The real delimits the void, whose differential opposite, [the phallus], on the graph of sexuation, attributes signifiers of having to being. These symbolize masculinity as a countable identity- that is, that which has value- in the symbolic sphere of public worth.
>
> (p. 66)

Those who do not identify with having the phallus, as previously mentioned, are left partially without signification. Their only option then, in order to participate in the Symbolic, is to identify with whatever instantiations of Woman are available at that particular socio-historical moment. Hence, the proliferation of discourses surrounding what it means to be a "real woman," which seemingly contradict one another, such as the Virgin/Whore dichotomy. This is why Lacan (1975) claims that Woman is a symptom of man, meaning that cultural representations and articulations identifying what it means to be a Woman rely on phallic representation of femininity. Feminine sexuation, then, in being an imaginary identification with the lack, is conceptualized as all that which evades the rules of the Symbolic, whereas masculine sexuation can be understood as a foreclosure of the Real (Ragland-Sullivan, 2004). How one obtains jouissance then, is determined by how the subject experiences the lack. Stevens (2007) clarifies that phallic jouissance on the masculine side is masturbatory in that it is imaginary and does not correspond to an other to rejoin with, but rather to a sexual object that will allow him sexual jouissance. This Other jouissance that women have access to is less localized in the body. This means love is implicated on the side of the feminine because it is a move away from this enjoyment of his or her own body and a move toward another.

The final consideration that must be identified as constituting sexuation is how the individual comes to understand the other sex, specifically, how they experience jouissance. The masturbatory enjoyment in phallic jouissance tends to posit the person on the feminine side as possessing his object a, or the objects that he enjoys and is gratified by. For the individual on the feminine side, love is fundamental to jouissance. Feminine jouissance, which I will elaborate on further, is "a relation to the not-whole part of the Other that allows for what Lacan calls the 'path of love' " (Barnard, 2002, p. 11). Similarly, Stevens (2007) argues that it is through the feminine, specifically the introduction of love, that "jouissance becomes civilized" (p. 218). While Lacan maintains that there is no relation between the sexes, that is, they cannot complete each other, or even completely satisfy each other's jouissance, love functions as a union between the sexes. In this union, the woman functions as the cause of the man's desire, and the man comes to realize the necessity of love in the union. An illusion is created by falling in love, which functions to assume a relation between the sexes. However, this illusion posits love as a necessity, which allows this relation to pass from an imaginary contingency to symbolic representation in the form of a symptom, or a metaphor originating in the Real (Stevens, 2007).

Sexuation, specifically in regard to the feminine positions for this book, then, denotes a way of coming to knowledge, rather than an imaginary or symbolic identification. Copjec (1994) explains that if sexuation is understood as a logic, then Lacan can be understood as replacing the terms "subject" and "predicate" in a proposition with "argument" and "function." She explains that the implication of this is that "male" and "female" are not groups to which certain descriptive attributes belong. Rather, one aligns with male or female based on how one situates oneself in relation to the function, meaning the enunciative position the individual assumes. This function, of course, is the phallic function, and it is either an affirmation or a negation of this function that determines either an inclusion or exclusion of absolute jouissance.

As mentioned, it is this formulation that allows Lacan to posit that there is no sexual relation. That is, there is no reconciling the fact that one half of the sexes has not taken up the signifier as a support for her subjective position.

As Zupančič (2017) claims, "One in the masculine position puts one's faith in the hands of the signifier, but one does not want to know what takes place in this swap [namely, 'castration']" (p. 52). As also mentioned earlier, this does not mean that woman is not castrated, as castration is the effect of all speaking beings. However, as Zupančič points out, the feminine side of sexuation seems to imply an exception to castration. She understands this in two ways,

> First, woman is "the Other, in the most radical sense, in the sexual relationship" [Lacan, 1999, p. 81]. And second, "there is no Other of the Other." If woman is the Other of man, man is not the Other of woman… In other words, the relationship to the Other is, so to speak, included in the Other, it is "part" of the Other. Whereas a man can think of the Other as the exception to the rule, to his rule, on the basis of which he relates to women, a woman cannot think of the Other as the exception to her rule, but as part of the rule, as included in the rule. This affects significantly the nature of this rule, making it "not-all."
>
> (p. 53)

What this comes to mean for the subject on the feminine side is that when the emergence of the Symbolic order coincides with the failure of one signifier to emerge, this gap opens up the potential for feminine jouissance—the signifier of the lack of knowledge in the Other (Zupančič, 2017, pp. 53–54). This is particularly important for the current project because it implies that feminine jouissance is not an obstacle to the sexual relation, but rather an indication that it does not exist. Enjoyment of the lack in the other threatens to expose that lack to that other, which phallic society and its participants of all genders have worked quite desperately to deny. In fact, it has been argued that the proliferation of gender identities is another way of denying lack (Kristeva, 1977; Zupančič, 2017), as any identity claim takes solace in a signifier as a subjective buffer. This is not a criticism of those advocating for the recognition and rights of gender identities that fall outside the binary. Symbolic representation should not be understood as somehow less real or vitally important. Rather, this should be heard as a consideration that may illuminate our persistence about making any sort of identity claim, as well as expose the ways in which we may fall into some of the same political and ideological dilemmas we sought to subvert. Instead, I suggest that it is not the establishment of new identities that may affect radical change in the sense that a change to the nature of subjectivity would have massive political implications, but rather that which has always managed to disturb the signifying order. That is to say that feminine jouissance, at the root of its nonexistence, threatens meaning, and meaning, specifically the establishment of I/Other dichotomy, has constituted subjectivity in the modern era.

While it has been argued that Lacan developed his theory of the feminine subject throughout his entire career (Soler, 2003), it is not until Seminar XX in 1975 in which Lacan dedicates a considerable amount of time to this topic. It is in this seminar that he makes the controversial claim that Woman does not exist. To demonstrate this point further, he challenges women to say more about their experience, suggesting that whatever the feminine experience might be, it will be inarticulable. Well-known feminist scholars have reacted against such a claim (Irigaray, 1985; Cixous, 2005), while others claim that Lacan has used psychoanalytic theory to explain what women have been suggesting about their role in the patriarchal order for years (Grosz, 1994; Braidotti, 2011). However, a careful examination of the claims Lacan makes about women is important in order to argue that the feminine has been suppressed and subsequently manifested in the monstrous.

By saying that Woman does not exist, Lacan is not claiming that there is no female subject, but rather that the very act of entering language is inherently phallic as demonstrated in his logic, and explicated earlier. For Lacan, sexual differentiation occurs in relation to the Real, and not via Symbolic articulations of what does or does not constitute difference (Copjec, 1994). Women are unable to fully represent their desires and experiences in the Symbolic due to its phallic (or patriarchal) nature, which means that whatever it means to be a Woman cannot be fully subjectified in the Symbolic. This means that there is a surplus remaining outside of language in the Real, or what he refers to as "not-all" (Lacan, 1975, p. 35). It is important to note that, for Lacan, women are not outside of the phallic order. Rather, they are frustratingly caught up in it as well, even if it fails to adequately signify for them. Attempts to lay claim to particular types of femininity or feminine identity are inherently phallic because of their reliance on signification, and the trading of signifiers in a phallic economy. However, because signifiers fail short, "Woman" is always in the Imaginary, constituted by uncanny perceptions, and subsequently subjected to disciplinary measures in an attempt to drain the Real. Furthermore, men are not necessarily outside of this "not-all" either, but rather they are more likely to progress through the Oedipus complex and be socialized in a way that accords to a fantasy that they in fact possess the phallus, and thus have the ability to circulate it within the Symbolic. Lacan (2006) reminds us that this is not true, and that no one possesses the phallus, but for men to participate in a patriarchal society that prides them on something they do not have, it behooves them to comply with the fantasy. As Soler (2003) points out, "Thanks to discourse, boys begin life with a little more capital: having the phallic signifier" (p. 50). Women, then, are left to contend with a double lack, which means a surplus.

It is this double lack that allows women access to another type of jouissance, what Lacan (1975) specifically called "feminine jouissance" and which he only began to work on at the end of his career. Because women are not adequately represented in the Symbolic, there are moments when they cannot fully participate in it, and because of this they are able to see what Bruce Fink (2002) referred to as "the fallibility of the phallic" (p. 37). In fact, Lacan also refers to this in the same seminar as "beyond the phallus" (Lacan, 1975). Feminine jouissance is the jouissance of the Other, that is, to be the jouissance of the Other, or to be enjoyed by the Other. This is likened to the experience of being the primary caregiver's phallus in early infancy with no separation between the subject and the Other. It is tempting to associate the Lacanian feminine with psychosis due to its similar identification of the Other (Fink, 1999), however, unlike in Lacanian psychosis, the woman is castrated, hence why her experience is in the form of fleeting jouissance, as opposed to a subjective structure. The role of the subject in this position, then, is to navigate the world of the Symbolic, which is founded on a law that rejects any apprehension of an outside to castration, and those experiences not mediated by castration that impinge and disturb the Symbolic.

Criticisms of Lacanian psychoanalysis

I cannot ignore the criticisms that Lacanian psychoanalysis or psychoanalysis in general have received, in particular by feminist scholars and theorists of sexual difference. Freudian psychoanalysis has been called sexist for its assertion that the development of the psyche is contingent on the presence or absence of the male sexual organ (Horney, 1967; Chodorow, 1989). Furthermore, Freud himself was accused of harboring sexist and oppressive beliefs about the young women he analyzed, and that he contributed to harmful gender stereotypes about women, such as having weak sensibilities, which was a causal factor in practices such as the rest cure. Similarly, Lacan has also been accused by scholars, such as Luce Irigaray and Judith Butler, of advocating his own brand of phallocentrism and a biological essentialism that reduces women to hysterics under male norms. Such criticisms allowed for the development of subsequently provocative and interesting theories regarding gender and sexual difference. As Grosz (1990) suggests, criticisms of the phallocentrism in Lacanian theory tend to focus extensively on his theories of the Symbolic and Imaginary registers, which is a problem as he considered sexual difference, or what he referred to as sexuation, in relation to the Real. These theories came later in his career, and it was much later when they were eventually translated into English, making such considerations only recently accessible to English-speaking critics.

However, feminist criticisms have lodged important challenges at psychoanalysis. Felman (1993), in her elaboration on Juliet Mitchell's defense of Freud, states that while psychoanalysis may provide a useful analysis of a patriarchal society, in which everything is in relation to the phallus, and woman is all that is not said, Freudian analysis is not entirely transparent to itself either. Furthermore, she argues that an outright rejection of feminist critique mirrors some of the feminist critiques of psychoanalysis, which are both premised in the same assumption: that the other fully knows what he or she says. Such a belief is incommensurate with psychoanalytic practice. Felman explains,

> The unconscious means that every insight is inhabited by its own blindness, which pervades it: you cannot simply polarize, oppose blindness and insight (whether such polarization then equates blindness with feminism and insight with psychoanalysis, or on the contrary puts the insight on the side of feminism and the blindness on the side of psychoanalytic theory).
>
> (p. 71)

Felman, as well as Grosz, attempts to articulate the space in between feminism and psychoanalysis, asking what each can offer the other. Psychoanalysts Julia Kristeva and Bracha Ettinger, among others, are examples of analysts who contribute to the dialogue between psychoanalysis and feminist critiques. It is my contention that psychoanalytic theory operating in conjunction with critical theory provides a necessary intervention in political discourses, demanding an account for the subject within the epistemic conditions.

Psychoanalysis and politics

The impetus to produce a psychoanalytic political praxis has been escalating in recent times. A number of scholars such as Slavoj Zizek, Ian Parker, Todd McGowan, Mari Ruti, Sheldon George, Derek Hook, and Stephanie Swales, to name a few have engaged with Lacanian psychoanalytic concepts to critique issues pertaining to capitalism, sexism, transgender phobia, and racism. For example, in his book on trauma and race, Sheldon George (2016) discusses how the unconscious perception of how the other enjoys, specifically how the other enjoys in relation to our lack, is a fundamental factor in issues of racism and racial identity in America. George suggests that assumptions that the other, in his example, African Americans, have found a way to fill their lack provokes anxiety about one's own lack, which leads to excessive reactions or attitudes directed at African Americans. Similarly, Derek Hook (2017) argues that jouissance is a political factor and worthy of political analysis due to the fact that jouissance, though it is unconscious, is intimately tied to the Symbolic and undergirds political acts, such as in the case of racism or sexism. Jouissance is a constituent in political praxis, and therefore those approaches that take its role seriously offer valuable insights into discourses and practices aimed at controlling, manipulating, and even accounting for the other, whoever that other may be. For feminist scholars interested in such discourses and practices aimed at women and feminine subjects, anxiety about possible Other or feminine jouissance is a useful starting point, with one possible identifying factor being that which is designated abject.

Kristeva and abjection

Since Seminar XX, scholars have taken a number of positions in regard to theorizing the feminine. Lacan's theories inherently critique any notion of a unified subject, while also posing questions about the nature of sexuality and the social order (Grosz, 1990). This makes his theories appealing to many feminist thinkers, not to mention Lacan's own provocation for women to say something of their experience (Lacan, 1975). Grosz (1990) refers to two such women, Julia Kristeva and Luce Irigaray, as the metaphorical daughters of Lacan, meaning that their own theories come directly from their contact with Lacanian theory. They each formulated their own theories of the feminine through a psychoanalytic framework. While Irigaray's theory is interesting in its own right, Grosz (1990) notes that Kristeva should be considered the "dutiful daughter" of Lacan and Freud, suggesting that she adheres more closely to their "law," whereas, Irigaray attempts to suggest an alternative position for women by beginning with the female body as the site of development (p. 150). Such a theory is valuable, but in remaining within the Lacanian tradition, offers a way to come to address the symptoms of the nonsexual rapport. Neither does an alternative view of the feminine subject addresses the tension and conflict the feminine subject encounters, nor does a new subjectivity premised on presence account for the lack therein. For this reason, Kristeva's adherence to Freud and Lacan, as well as her notions of semiotics and the abject lend themselves more naturally to a consideration of ostracized femininity. Kristeva's critique of the feminist movement is also worth noting. Feminist projects, as she understood them, sought to claim power for women within a bourgeois state, and failed to consider the way in which the Law repeated itself in the feminist agenda. She echoes Lacan's concern, in which as soon as the subject speaks, she submits herself to the phallic law (Moi, 1986). She states,

> At the moment, this is all there is, and that's not bad. But will there be more? A different relationship of the subject to discourse, to power? Will the eternal frustration of the hysteric in relation to discourse oblige the latter to reconstruct itself? Will it give rise to unrest in everybody, male or female? Or will it remain a cry outside time, like the great mass movements that break up the old system, but have no problem in submitting to the demands of order, as long as it is a new order?
>
> (Kristeva, 1977, p. 511)

Kristeva does not deviate from Lacan's theory of the Symbolic, but rather provides an addendum. She suggested that signification is composed of both the symbolic and the semiotic. The symbolic is the structure and grammar that govern the ways in which language provides meaning, which is similar to Lacan's early notion of the Symbolic (Grosz, 1990). Semiotics, on the other hand, are the discharges of the bodily drives via the tones and rhythmic elements of language (Oliver, 2002). Grosz (1990) explains that the semiotic "can be correlated with the anarchic pre-oedipal component-drives, and polymorphous erotogenic zones, orifices, and organs ... it is the raw material of all signification" (pp. 150–151). The symbolic can be said to be the law, in the Lacanian sense, which channels this libidinal force into articulation for the purposes of communication and relationality.

For Kristeva, the semiotic is a component of the feminine, to which I will add "of sexuation." She argues that the semiotic, loaded with infantile drives, is presymbolic, therefore precastration and in direct relation to the space of the mother's body. Kristeva follows Plato and designates this space as the semiotic chora (Kristeva, 1969). She notes that "the chora, as rupture and articulations (rhythm), precedes evidence, verisimilitude, spatiality and temporality. Our discourse- all discourse- moves with and against the chora in the sense that it simultaneously depends upon and refuses it" (Kristeva, 1986, p. 94). This space is both presymbolic and pre-imaginary and thus becomes a space that both defines the limits of the body, and therefore the ego, which subverts the subject. It is the space in which the death drive, that is, the compulsion to repeat, first manifests and threatens to destroy the emerging subject, which can be understood as the jouissance of the Other. It is important to note here that though Kristeva identified this space as conceptually feminine, she remains faithful to Freud and Lacan in maintaining that the mother is always phallic, meaning that she is the product of the masculine fantasy, as opposed to any sort of phenomenological experience of her maternity or as a woman (Grosz, 1990). To reiterate, in contrast to the maternal orientation of the semiotic, the symbolic is similar to the Lacanian symbolic, in that it is oedipalized, and subject to the Law of the Father (Kristeva, 1986). The semiotic can be said to press up against the Symbolic, returning via irruptions, such as an interruption or dissonance in the rhythm of the otherwise rational or logical flow of speech. It is by its nature excessive, which is why Kristeva (1969) points to "madness, holiness and poetry" as the site of semiotic subversion (p. 64).

In her later works, Kristeva (1982) returns to the feminine to discuss the abject and abjection in *Powers of horror: An essay on abjection*. The abject and its relation to the feminine nature of semiotics are pertinent to the current consideration of the subjugation of the feminine into monstrosity. Kristeva's formulations of the abject rely on the work of Mary Douglas (1966), in which Douglas discusses the cultural connotations of dirt and purity and what constitutes the difference between the clean, the unclean, and the sacred. Kristeva (1982) argues that the abject is not just what we typically consider unclean or grotesque, but rather that which threatens our status as a subject. It is both horrifying and mesmerizing. Furthermore, abjection is a process that infants must pass through in order to become a subject, whereby the infant will understand the mother's body as abject. This provides an impetus to escape the jouissance of the Other and subsequently become motivated to move away from the mother's body in order to become a subject. How this occurs is different among the sexes. Oliver (2002) explains that the male child experiences horror due to his dependence on the mother's body as he weans, while simultaneously fascinated by it, allowing for an eroticization of the female body. Kristeva (1982) describes this as a splitting of the mother into the sublime and the terrifying. Females, however, do not split the mother, but rather unsuccessfully try to rid themselves of her, leading Kristeva to construe feminine sexuality as a melancholic sexuality.

This theory of abjection runs contrary to Lacan's formation of the subject as the result of castration threats. She argues, rather, that the infant does not simply take the mother's body as her first object, but rather is engaged in an identification and separation process long before the mirror stage or castration (Oliver, 2002). Furthermore, Kristeva also challenges Freud's (1939) assumption that society is organized around the murder of the father, arguing instead that there is a repression of the feminine, specifically maternal authority. National and cultural identity is constructed similarly to the subject, in which the feminine must be excluded in order for any sort of individual ego to develop (Oliver, 2002). My argument deviates slightly, suggesting that the feminine is sublimated into various types of manifestations of the monstrous because it contradicts the Law of the Father, as expressed in the epistemic logic, and subsequently the structure of the subject.

Radical subjectivity: Deleuze and Guattari

It is not enough, however, to just consider these different instantiations of sexual difference or attacks that attempt to limit the jouissance of the Other. To do so would fail to consider the ways in which these manifestations change throughout different historical epochs, but more importantly, what effect they may have had. To do this, I turn to Deleuze and Guattari, specifically their texts *A thousand plateaus* (1980), as well as *Anti-Oedipus* (1972) to consider the latent potential these encounters may have had in challenging the rigid structures of modernist subjectivity, specifically Oedipalized subjectivity. To fully understand what this means and how it could be considered within the context of this book, a brief explication of some of the major concepts in Deleuze and Guattari's philosophy is needed, as is a consideration of the points in which Lacan and the authors of his scathing critique could be said to address or build on one another.

Similar to Lacanian theory, a complete, and even altogether coherent, reiteration of Deleuze and Guattari's philosophies is not tenable here. Instead, I will follow Deleuze's advice and adopt a rhizomatic approach to the scope of their work, diving in where and when I find the most productive for the current project. In doing so, I consider the ways in which certain parts of their theories work in conjunction with Lacanian analysis, without necessarily needing to reconcile the many disparate notions with Lacanian analysis. I would like to first consider the Deleuzian project, before briefly turning to some of the contentions between Deleuze and Guattari and Lacan. Gilles Deleuze was a French philosopher who paired up with Lacanian psychoanalyst Felix Guattari to write *Anti-Oedipus: Capitalism and schizophrenia* following the events of May 1968 (Nedoh and Zevnik, 2016).

Central to their theory is challenging the static nature of subjectivity, conceptualized as "being" and instead offer an approach premised in becoming. Grounded heavily in Spinozist philosophy, becoming is a move toward a nonrepresentational subject, such that the term "subject" would no longer be appropriate. Identities predicated on becoming are understood as assemblages and are thus designed as such to be in flux, rather than whole or essential. For Deleuze, privileging becoming over being more adequately understands reality as perpetual processes and repetitions of difference (Tiessen, 2012). Furthermore, becomings are constituted as either molar or molecular, with any assemblage being composed of both (Deleuze and Guattari, 1980). King (2012) explained that molar refers to distinct edges and boundaries that denote particular objects or identities, and those things and beings that are heavily coded as wholes. On the other hand, molecular assemblages are what support the molar assemblages, and are characterized by their openness, dynamism, and multiplicities. This is not to say that one is either molar or molecular, but rather we are constantly oscillating through molar and molecular becomings with different degrees of freedom. The project for Deleuze and Guattari is to move toward opening up more degrees of freedom, so that subjectivity itself does not become a fascist practice. They understand molarization of identity occurring in a variety of texts, Lacanian psychoanalysis notably one of them, but for the purposes of this book, I will stick with their concerns regarding gender and sexual difference.

Massumi (1992) notes that Deleuze and Guattari do not argue against sexual difference. Rather, they argue that gender is a molar identity that increasingly offers less and less fluidity or opportunities for experimentation. In particular, they note that the identity constituted as "man" has been overcoded and thus, is closed off to experimentation. This does not necessarily contrast with the Lacanian interpretation, as the masculine subject is the castrated subject who refers to a masculine-ideal, or a subject who has not been castrated and enjoys perfectly. This perception sets the subject on a subjective loop of habitual jouissance. For Deleuze and Guattari, in order to engage with a molecular becoming, one has to move away from man, and toward becoming-other. Becoming-other is considered in three distinct modes—becoming-woman, becoming-child, and becoming-animal. These should not be understood as the only modes of becoming, but rather those that immediately lend themselves to a molecular, minoritarian identity formation, that is, those which have not been adequately matriculated into the social order, and because of this, their identities have been susceptible to the changing signifiers.

Becoming-woman

Deleuze and Guattari (1980) reiterate that becoming-woman is not to be confused with the molar identity of woman, who is defined by her form and function as constituted by the gender roles and norms within a given time period. They elaborate by saying that "the woman as a molar entity has to become-woman in order that the man also become- or can become-woman" (p. 276). They argue that all becomings must first pass through becoming-woman, as it is "the key to all becomings" (p. 277). To elucidate further, becoming-woman, they claim

> must first be understood as a function of something else: not imitating or assuming the female form, but emitting particles that enter the relation of movement and rest, or the zone of proximity, of a microfemininity, in other words, that produce in us a molecular woman, create the molecular woman.
>
> (p. 275)

Becoming-woman challenges the duality of gendered bodies by occupying a space in between, composed in fluidity, characteristic of their machinic assemblages. They identify Virginia Woolf as an example of someone who uses her writing to become-woman, claiming that she was appalled at the idea of writing as a woman. Instead, they argue "writing should produce a becoming-woman as atoms of womanhood capable of crossing and impregnating them up in that becoming" (p. 276). They go on to suggest that the reason that there is potential in becoming-woman is because the woman's body is first overcoded and imposed upon with rigid rules and a history of what her body has meant. Subsequently, a history is also foisted on the body of the boy, but it is always in relation to the girl's, and so the girl serves as an example and a trap, through which she is both victim and object of his desire, a prepubescent femme fatale. Becoming-woman then does not rely on the molarized body of the woman, but rather the space between bodies that calls into question the supposed discrete boundaries of self/other, male/female. Deleuze and Guattari demonstrate this when they elaborate on Virginia Woolf and claim that no man has been spared from this rise of women writers, "even those who pass for the most virile, the most phallocratic, such as Lawrence and Miller, in their turn continually tap into and emit particles that enter the proximity or zone of indiscernibility of women" (p. 276). Becoming-woman is an encounter, though instantaneous, prevalent, and even surreptitious.

Becoming-woman relies on a particular understanding of what constitutes, or what I argue fails to constitute, the woman. There are assumptions implicit in Deleuze and Guattari's understanding of becoming-woman that seem to draw on Lacan's understanding that the woman does not exist. Becoming-woman, due to the woman's perpetual position as not-man from which man understands himself to be and subsequently overcoded by, is almost indistinguishable from the Lacanian dilemma of the woman as lacking signification. To reiterate, if the term "woman" is a signifier, which is phallic, it never fully accounts for that which it attempts to signify. This in turn leads to "woman" always being constituted in relation to a shifting signifier, that is, whatever is not man.

This is where Lacan stops, specifically because of his understanding that this sexual difference is inherently tied to the Real and more specifically jouissance. As Zupančič (2017) points out, for Lacan, "the Real is not some realm or substance to be talked about, it is the inherent contradiction of speech, twisting its tongue, so to speak" (pp. 68–69). This is why Lacan cheekily incites women to say something about this Other jouissance, admitting that not only he is unable given his level of castration, but also that they cannot either because the very nature of it refuses utterance. Furthermore, this Other jouissance can be found in the speaking itself, in which signification is not the intended goal. Lacan uses James Joyce as an example of someone who speaks from this jouissance. This is also why it is difficult from a Lacanian perspective to say something about this Other jouissance, as to speak about something is to come to a stopping point. Furthermore, for Lacan, there is no way to make a metalanguage of the Real. This is where Zupančič identifies the role of equivocation in psychoanalysis, in which the analyst borrows signifiers from the analysand, not to precisely name the conflict in a cinematic perversion of the Freudian clinic, but rather to move that which cannot be spoken.

It could be argued here that Deleuze and Guattari take up Lacan's assertion of Woman and this Other jouissance in a way that Lacan is unable to due to his ties to the clinic. This is unfair and misses how the theorists can be used in a collaborative project such as this. It can instead be argued that Deleuze and Guattari form an ontology of the Real, whereby Lacan does not. In refusing to form an ontology of the Real, Lacanian analysts instead work with the subject's jouissance as it pertains to each subject's neurotic or psychotic position. From this perspective, the subject is privileged. However, in making an ontology of the Real, Deleuze and Guattari neutralize the Real as a means to speculate and facilitate contact with it in a way that considers and produces change. This corresponds to a political project in which the very nature of subjectivity is at the heart of political discourse, in which the nature of the human subject is not a taken for granted assumption, but one which has undergone shifts in relation to the dominant systems' ideologies, technologies of biopower, and methods of subjectivization (Foucault, 1973). Lacan would agree with this, although as Zupančič points out, Lacan would be reluctant to create his own ontology of the Real, not because he believes that psychoanalysis is exempt from interrogation, but rather

> the very notion of ontology has to be expanded by an additional concept (the Real) that holds and marks the place of its inherent contradiction/impossibility. And the subject is the effect of this contradiction, not an offshoot of being. There is the subject because there is the Real.
>
> (p. 119)

This is one of the biggest discrepancies between Lacan and Deleuze and I would be remiss to not mention it. Deleuze, and many of the materialist theories that have been established in a Deleuzian tradition, rely on a radical desubjectivation and question the ways in which habitual forms of subjectivation enslave desire and the body. This is not to say that Deleuze and Guattari would argue that one can apprehend the Real in a way that produces a desired effect, but rather that there can be an awareness of the Real that apprehends the potential for experimentation.

One way to work productively with this disconnect regarding the Real is to consider the feminist materialists', specifically Rosi Braidotti's, critique, of Deleuze's notion of becoming-woman. Braidotti suggests that in positing becoming-woman as a juncture for all becomings to pass through on their way toward a multiplicity, while simultaneously calling for its dismissal, attempts to bypass phallocentric representation on the promise of something new, without properly contending with sexual difference as a metaphysical and epistemological difference. She also claims that it is dangerous for one to diffuse a sexuality that has already historically been coded as dark and mysterious (Braidotti, 2011). To contend with this, she advocates for a return to the body and affect as the site to develop an approach she refers to as nomadic subjectivity. It is my intention to remain largely within the psychoanalytic tradition as a means to consider how one can become-woman when woman is always that which is not Woman. I would argue that even in identifying with a particular instantiation of Woman at any given time, is to move toward further phallicization, which is what Deleuze also seems to be arguing. However, identification on the side of the woman in Lacanian psychoanalysis is always premised in a masquerade, that is, in a disguise that positions the woman as a fully castrated woman. To follow Zupančič, "the essence of femininity is to pretend to be a woman. One is a woman if one carries castration as a mask" (p. 55). It would be a mistake, however, to read this as a sort of agentic move on the part of the subject, but rather a necessity that keeps the subject speaking and acting, as well as produces a buffer from the anxiety of noncastration. In order to do this, as well as take Braidotti's claims against Deleuze's notions of sexual difference seriously, I look specifically at those cases that posit specific women at the sight of this questioning who are being interrogated following some sort of disturbance that demonstrated the era's authoritative knowledge inability to adequately account for her desire. This allows me not to speculate about all women in some sort of essentialist claim, but rather analyze those points of anxiety about difference, as well as consider what the latent potential those encounters may have for rethinking subjectivity. Furthermore, it is this anxiety, serving as surplus, both on the side of the woman, as well as those who encounter her, that I explore further as first the site of the nonsexual relation, as well as a consideration of how this could potentially open onto an arena for an exploration of becoming-woman.

By strategically laying out the elements of Lacanian theory alongside Deleuze and Guattari's notion of becoming-woman, and using Braidotti's critique to thread them together, I have fashioned a means with which to consider sexual difference and reactions to it as a phenomenon that cannot be adequately encapsulated in discourses that fail to account for the unconscious. However, it is not my intention to reconcile these theorists, nor is it necessarily my intention to collapse one into the other for a more holistic theory. Rather, following Nedoh and Zevnik's (2016) project, I seek to build a disjunctive bridge. A disjunctive bridge, though seemingly ineffective can be thought of the necessary construction of what has come and what shall come, with a gap in the middle. This gap, central to Lacanian theory, is where knowledge is produced.

References

Barnard, S. (2002). Introduction. In S. Barnard and B. Fink's (Eds.), *Reading seminar xx: Lacan's major work on love, knowledge and feminine sexuality* (1–20). Albany, NY: State University of New York Press.

Braidotti, R. (2011). *Nomadic subjects: Embodiment and sexual difference in contemporary feminist theory.* New York: Columbia University Press.

Butler, J. (1990). *Gender trouble: Feminism and the subversion of identity.* New York: Routledge.

Chodorow, N. (1989). *Feminism and psychoanalytic theory*. Oxford: Polity Press.
Cixous, H. (2005). *Stigmata: Escaping texts*. New York: Routledge.
Copjec, J. (1994). *Read my desire: Lacan against the historicists*. Chicago, IL: Verso Press.
Deleuze, G. and Guattari, F. (1972). *Anti-oeidpus: Capitalism and schizophrenia*. London: Penguin Classics.
Deleuze, G. and Guattari, F. (1980). *A thousand plateaus: Capitalism and schizophrenia*. Minneapolis, MN: University of Minnesota Press.
Douglas, M. (1966). *Purity and danger*. New York: Routledge.
Felman, S. (1993). *What does a woman want? Reading and sexual difference*. Baltimore, MD: The John Hopkins University Press.
Fink, B. (1996). *The Lacanian subject: Between language and jouissance*. Princeton, NJ: Princeton University Press.
Fink, B. (1999). *A clinical introduction to Lacanian psychoanalysis: Theory and technique*. New York: Routledge.
Fink, B. (2002). Knowledge and jouissance. In S. Barnard's and B. Fink's (Eds.), *Reading seminar xx: Lacan's major work on love, knowledge, and feminine sexuality* (11–45). Albany, NY: State University of New York.
Freud, S. (1939). *Moses and monotheism*. New York: Knopf Publishers.
Foucault, M. (1982). The subject and power. In H.L. Dreyfus and P. Rabinow's (Eds.) *Foucault: Beyond hermeneutics and structuralism* (208–226). Brighton: Harvester.
George, S. (2016). *Trauma and race: A Lacanian study on African American racial identity*. Waco, TX: Baylor University Press.
Grosz, E. (1990). *Jacques Lacan: A feminist introduction*. London: Routledge.
Grosz, E. (1994). *Volatile bodies: Towards a corporeal feminism*. Bloomington, IN: Indiana University Press.
Hook, D. (2017). What is "enjoyment as a political factor?" *Political Psychology*, 4 (38), 605–620.
Horney, K. (1967). *Feminine psychology*. New York: W.W. Norton & Co.
Irigaray, L. (1985). *Speculum of the other woman*. Ithaca, NY: Cornell University Press.
King, R.D. (2012). Molar/molecular. In R. Shields and M. Vallee (Eds.), *Demystifying Deleuze: An introductory assemblage of crucial concepts* (117–119). Ottawa: Quill Books.
Kristeva, J. (1969). *Desire in language: A semiotic approach to literature and art*. New York: Columbia University Press.
Kristeva, J. (1977). *Polylogue*. Paris: Editions du Seuil.
Kristeva, J. (1982). *Powers of horror: An essay on abjection*. New York: Columbia University Press.
Kristeva, J. (1986). *The Kristeva reader*. T. Moi (Ed.). New York: Columbia University Press.
Lacan, J. (1975). Of structure as an inmixing of an otherness prerequisite to any subject whatever. In R. Macksey and E. Donato's (Eds.), *The structuralist controversy: The language of criticisms and the sciences of man* (186–200). Baltimore, MD: John Hopkins University Press.
Lacan, J. (2006). *Ecrits: The complete first edition in English*. New York: W.W. Norton & Co.

Levy-Stokes, C. (2001). Jouissance. In H. Glowinski, Z.M. Marks and S. Murphy's (Eds.), *A compendium of Lacanian terms* (101–109). London: Free Association Books.
Mark, Z.M. (2001). Object a. In H. Glowinski, Z.M. Marks and S. Murphy's (Eds.), *A compendium of Lacanian terms* (122–129). London: Free Association Books.
Massumi, B. (1992). *A user's guide to capitalism and schizophrenia: Deviations from Deleuze and Guattari.* Cambridge: The MIT Press.
Moi, T. (1986). Introduction. In T. Moi's (Ed.), *The Kristeva reader* (1–22). New York: Columbia University Press.
Nedoh, B. and Zevnik, A. (2016). *Lacan and Deleuze: A disjunctive synthesis.* Edinburgh: Edinburgh University Press.
Oliver, K. (2002). *The portable Kristeva.* New York: Columbia University Press.
Ragland-Sullivan, E. (2004). *The logic of sexuation: From Aristotle to Lacan.* Albany, NY: State University of New York Press.
Soler, C. (2003). *What Lacan said about women: A psychoanalytic study.* New York: Other Press.
Soler, C. (2014). *Lacan: The unconscious reinvented.* London: Karnac Books Ltd.
Stevens, A. (2012). Love and sex beyond identifications. In V. Veroz and B. Wolf's (Eds.), *The later Lacan: An introduction* (211–221). Albany, NY: State University of New York Press.
Tiessen, M. (2012). Becoming. In R. Shields and M. Vallee (Eds.), *Demystifying Deleuze: An introductory assemblage of crucial concepts* (33–36). Ottawa: Red Quill Books.
Vanier, A. (2000). *Lacan.* New York: Other Press.
Zupančič, A. (2017). *What is sex?* Cambridge: The MIT Press.

Chapter 3

Sexual difference in mythology

> So God created humankind in His image, in the image of God He created them; male and female He created them.
>
> (Genesis 1:27)

One of the most accessible resources for discourses about sexual difference is in the form of myth and literature. For my purposes here, those myths and stories that are concerned with the feminine as monstrous can potentially shed light on assumptions about the ways in which the other might enjoy, and how that enjoyment could be perceived as threatening the solitude of knowledge that castration produced. By utilizing specific examples from Christian and Greek mythology, questions about sexual difference that bleed from the pages of texts and into the practices and attitudes toward women of that era will be considered. This can be seen in two specific practices during the Middle Ages: the persecution of witches and the dissection of the bodies of some mystics after their deaths. This chapter should not be considered an exhaustive review of such material, but rather an illustrative example of the ways in which myth can inform discourse, which can then inform practice. These discourses can then provide fodder for speculations about the unconscious motivations underlying the representation and treatment of feminine monstrosity. This will then allow for a consideration for the ways becoming-woman might provide an opportunity to mine these encounters for their potential to open the subject in a given assemblage up to a line of flight, in which these notions of sexual difference no longer restrict ideas of the subject in the way that they did prior to the encounter.

Monstrous-feminine in myth

Feminine monsters are scattered throughout and across many different cultural myths, with each culture having their own distinct version. However, it seems to be consistent that the monsters that could be identified as feminine seem to possess traits that either emphasize or pervert their femininity. This follows what Creed (1993) illustrated with feminine monsters in contemporary horror movies mentioned in Chapter 1. While it could be argued that gender norms and assumptions about the female body prohibit storytellers and artists from endowing feminine monsters with the same brute strength or inclination toward weapons, there also tends to be something else, something not easily apprehended in the portrayal, but which seems to be at the center of their monstrousness. I would like to suggest that latent in these representations of feminine monsters is a question about how women enjoy or about other jouissance. More specifically, there seems to be a question about feminine desire that cannot be satisfied via the phallus. I will focus on three of the more popular examples in Greek mythology, Medusa and the Gorgon sisters, the Sphinx, and Sirens, as a way to discuss how there seem to be unconscious questions, which cannot be adequately articulated, resonate, and reverberate in popular and enduring myths. Furthermore, the fact that these examples have endured and are recreated in stories and films today suggest that there is still a trace of a question about what these monsters have (or enjoy) that their masculine counterparts may not.

Medusa is a well-known and important figure in both psychoanalysis (Freud, 1922) and feminist theory (Cixous, 1992). To state it briefly, Medusa was one of three sisters, all of which were supposedly quite beautiful. Poseidon, the temperamental god of the sea fell in love with her; however, she would not return his love. She was punished by being turned into a monster with live snakes in her hair, along with her three sisters. However, her face was left beautiful, but looking upon it would turn the spectator to stone. Perseus, founder of Mycenae and on his own hero's journey, was instructed to kill her, which he accomplished by looking at Medusa's reflection in order to behead her and avoid being turned to stone and decapitated her. He gave the head to Athena, the goddess of wisdom and defender of Athens (Wilk, 2014), who in other (Ovid, 2014) versions of the tale was actually the one who turned Medusa into a monster out of jealousy after she saw Poseidon rape her in her temple. Regardless, the myth emphasizes that Medusa was in possession of something that moved or provoked the onlooker.

In *Beyond the pleasure principle*, Freud (1922) suggested that the story of Medusa was a simple one to interpret, with her decapitated head reminiscent of castration anxiety in males. Freud argued that the site of female genitalia, usually his mother's, is horrific to the young boy, who until this point was not confronted with the reality of castration. The hair surrounding the mother's genitalia, similar to the frightening snake-hair of Medusa, intervenes as a phallic symbol, that is premised in presence, and the onlooker turns to stone, which of course should be read here as becomes erect, thus reinforcing the belief that he is still in possession of his own phallus.

Similarly, sirens were also considered dangerous for their seductive powers. Sirens were said to possess female bodies with wings and would supposedly play beautiful music with lyres and harps near the ocean's shores. This music was said to be so beautiful that it would captivate the passing sailors, forcing them to wreck on the rocky shores. Though sirens make appearances throughout literature, the most well-known encounter with sirens was Odysseus's in Homers' (1997) *Odyssey*. The sailors were instructed to not listen to the songs of the sirens, lest they succumb to their own deaths. Odysseus, curious about what the songs sounded like, instructed his crew to plug their ears and tie him to a mast. When the ship passed the sirens, Odysseus begged to be freed in order to follow the music, but his crew, upon being instructed prior, only tied him tighter to the mast until they were out of range from the beguiling music. It is suggested that the sirens, having failed to lead a mortal to his death, threw themselves into the raging water to perish.

In each of these examples, Medusa and the sirens are said to possess something that the mortals, more specifically the male mortals, are unable to turn away from despite that their seduction will be the thing that will most certainly kill them. As Creed points out, death by seduction is most clearly exemplified in the case of Medusa, in which the men's desire for her leads to their petrification. She suggests that it is not that Medusa represented castration and that was what elicited the terror from her victims, but rather that she will castrate. This idea, though interesting, fails to acknowledge the Lacanian conceptualization of castration as the split between the self and the Other, which allows the subject to become a subject. I would like to suggest instead that the terror that Medusa evoked is rather in her ability to provoke an unconscious threat to refuse to acknowledge castration and thus return the subject to the jouissance of the Other, and in such, feminizing the subject. This is not to say that being a feminine subject is inherently monstrous, but rather from the position of a castrated subject, who has an unconscious assumption about the nature of sexual difference and how the Other enjoys, combined with castration anxiety of losing what he never had, to become feminized in this context is to be consumed, enjoyed, and devoured. It is a loss of subjectivity, at least partially.

Similarly, the sirens seem to suggest that there may be something alluring about this ultimate destruction of subjectivity. In the case of Odysseus, he desperately wants to hear the music. This curiosity, what Lacan would call desire, leads him dangerously close to the cause of his desire. That is, it seems that in the music of the sirens, he found his object a. The description of his face contorting along with his pleas to be let go so he can join them suggests a confrontation with the Real in all of its painful glory. Similar to the myth of Medusa and Perseus, one's imagination does not have to wander far to understand the allusions to orgasmic ecstasy suggested in Odysseus's experience. Furthermore, the fact that it is music that lures sailors is interesting for questions about sexual difference. It is not that the sirens are so beautiful, but rather that they communicate in a way that lies outside language but have a resonating and affecting character within the Symbolic, despite, according to Kristeva (1969), being intimately tied to the Real.

The link between sexual difference and knowledge is more clearly explicated in the myth of the Greek sphinx. Unlike the Egyptian sphinx, the Greek sphinx had a lion body, wings, a serpent-headed tail, and a female head. Her job was to guard the passage to the city of Thebes. Travelers who wanted to enter had to first answer her riddle, and if they did not, she would kill them. The most famous version of the riddle is found in the myth of Oedipus Rex, which was "Which creature has one voice and yet becomes four-footed and two-footed and three-footed?" (Sophocles, 1991). Supposedly, Oedipus was the only one able to solve the riddle, the answer of course being "man."

The myth of the sphinx demonstrates the link between knowledge and sexual difference most clearly of all because her riddle demands a certain type of signifier. However, the supposed choice of signifier is perhaps the most interesting of all. The answer, "man" both a phallic word and a word pointing to the phallus, suggests that she required the appropriate signifier as an answer to her question predicated on her desire. However, if "man" is understood not as he who has the phallus, but rather "Man" as in "Being" then a subtle hint is placed as to how the author has believed the sphinx has been enjoying sexually the whole time—by consuming men. The answer to her riddle is what prevents her from consuming any further. She must take the signifier at its word, so to speak. What makes this even more provocative is that the person who offered her the signifier, Oedipus, is the same character who, in Freud's approximation, fails to escape his mother's enjoyment. In what is usually interpreted as an accomplishment by Oedipus for having what the Other needed in order for her to end her reign of terror, which in some versions of the myth she was grateful for, also contains within it an implicit assumption about how woman enjoys—by consuming.

What is interesting about these myths is that there is an unassimilable part about the feminine monsters that lies at the juncture of what seduces the mortals and what kills them. Freud suggested in his analysis of the Medusa myth that Medusa's head was a metaphor for the mother's genitals, meaning that which has provided evidence of castration. Creed points out that Medusa marks the difference of feminine sexuality, noting that the fact that Medusa's onlookers would become stiff with terror and turn to stone was not lost on Freud. Creed also identifies sirens in the beginning pages of her text, alongside her comments about Medusa, as characters which seem to evoke terror for the fact that they represent difference. I would like to push this claim a bit further and suggest that this difference lies within it a question about what one has for the Other, specifically how does the Other enjoy sexually if she does not need the phallus (that one does not have to give her regardless). In each of these myths, there seems to be a trick of sorts in order to outwit the female monsters. To reiterate, I am not as concerned with the metaphor, but what is implicit in these depictions, and what fails to be accounted for when the monster is slain or outwitted.

Women in the Bible

While Greek mythology had a large effect on literature, art, and film, the Christian Bible was and is used as a guide for best practices in many scenarios, sexual difference being one of them. While most religions and religious texts have notorious evil villains, many notably female, I will limit my analysis to a few from the Old Testament because of the prominent influence the Bible has had on Western civilization. The figure of Woman has occupied an interesting place within the Bible, which has sparked many commentaries and analysis. The figures of Eve and Lilith have received considerable attention from feminist scholars and I would like to return to them as not only a means first to demonstrate the ways questions about sexual difference are implicit in their depictions, but also to then use them as a bridge between literature and the practices that began to have an actual effect on the bodies of once-living women.

To summarize a well-known figure quickly, Eve is found in the Garden of Eden, according to the Book of Genesis. In some accounts, she is the first human woman, wife of Adam and made from his rib. Adam and Eve were created by God and lived in the Garden of Eden, where all of their desires were satisfied, and they lived naked among the animals in perfect harmony. However, the Garden of Eden also contained tree of knowledge, which was forbidden by God to eat from. However, while Adam is briefly absent, in some accounts, this is because he was allegedly flirting with the angels (Milton, 2003), Eve is seduced by a serpent in the tree who convinces her to eat from the tree. Adam, following Eve's lead, also eats from the tree. Consuming the fruit allows them to possess knowledge, but with that knowledge comes shame and evil. As their punishment, they are banished from the Garden of Eden, damning humanity with them. They must bear the burden of humiliation, becoming embarrassed by their own naked bodies, and Eve, being the instigator, condemns herself and all womankind to endure painful childbirth.

In contrast, Lilith makes a number of different appearances in the Bible, but her relationship to Adam and Eve is a speculation among Hebrew scholars. According to these scholars, it states in Genesis that Adam had a wife before Eve, who they believe to be Lilith. Genesis states, "And God created man in His image, in the image of God He created him; male and female He created them" (1:27–28). This led to theories that the woman that was created in God's image was not Eve, as she is made from Adam's rib (Cohen, 2006). It has been suggested that Lilith left Adam and the Garden of Eden because she refused to become subservient to him (Kvam, Schearing, Linda, and Ziegler, 1999). Lilith also makes appearances throughout Jewish literature and folklore as some form of demon. Some depictions, such as in the Babylonia Talmud, describe her as a dangerous and promiscuous night demon, who had the propensity to steal babies (Hammer, 2017).

This is the version of her in the Babylonian Talmud, which has given rise to numerous pieces of art and literature of the night demon.

While both Eve and Lilith have been written about extensively in a number of disciplines, their myths demonstrate the ways in which sexual difference has been commonly depicted, which then manifests in assumptions and practices toward women. Though there are many other women who make appearances throughout different versions of the bibles, these two are of particular interest not only because of the question about their relationship, but also because they are both representations of fallen women depicted within a very pervasive Law in Western civilization. In the case of Eve, central to her character, is her inability to resist temptation. However, the nature of the temptation is what is interesting when considering other jouissance. Eating from the tree promised her knowledge, which suggests that implicit in this illustration of Eve as the first woman is a question about what she must desire, when at her feet already seems to lie perfect enjoyment. The Garden of Eden, constituted as perfection in which all needs are supposedly met, is not enough for Eve. If Eden is understood as representing the Symbolic, operating under the paternal metaphor of God's Law, it is important that it is Eve who is the first to transgress. It is helpful to remember here that subjects operate within the Symbolic as if signifiers always correspond to a signified, and though they do not, this common sense is what allows for certain types of knowledge to be produced. While this act could be read as a sexist depiction of woman, in that she is responsible for the fall of humanity and the cause of original sin in humankind, it also suggests that even in a supposed perfect Symbolic order, the desire of the Woman is not accounted for, thus undermining the nature of a perfect Symbolic order in the first place. Kristeva (1982) takes this notion up as well in her discussion on the abject and the Bible. Following her argument that subjects are split through abjection and must find resolve for this split in order to participate in the Symbolic, she further posits that the story of original sin in Christianity finds its abreaction in the consumption of communion as Christ's body. She states that because Christianity identified abjection as a fantasy of devouring, "Henceforth reconciled with it, the Christian subject, completely absorbed into the Symbolic, is no longer a being of abjection but a lapsing subject" (p. 119). Eve, then in devouring the spoiled fruit, the abject fruit, is answered with a Symbolic act of devouring—a stand in for the male body, the phallus, which cut the jouissance of the Other.

The myth surrounding Lilith provides further speculation regarding the desire of Woman, which coincides with this logic. If Lilith was made in the image of God (the Law) and if she was somehow either corruptible or refused to remain in the Garden of Eden, there arises a question about the nature of a "perfect woman." If the Woman does not exist according to Lacan because of the inability of the Symbolic to account for her, and Lilith is made in the image of God, then it would stand to reason that she must be the instantiation of Woman. The debate about her existence in Eden, and the subsequent myths regarding her seem to posit a question about how a Woman could exist in Eden in the first place. If Eve is the representation of a partially castrated feminine subject, being born from a rib rather than in the image of God, and she is tempted with what lies outside of Eden, Lilith's seemingly nonexistence in Eden has different implications that go beyond debates about interpretation. It is not so much whether or not there was a wife before Eve, but could there exist a Woman at all. While some seem to suggest that she was there and banished, and others claiming she was never there in the first place, Lilith's appearances in a number of other places, including the Bible and folklore, offer insight to the unconscious questions about what she may have found outside of Eden, and for our purposes here, the Symbolic order. It is not a coincidence that she is accused with stealing babies, and that babies, according to Freud (2010) allow women to have their own phallus. Lilith, unable to ascertain her own phallus, consumes the already tenable phallic instantiation for other women, so that her very presence evokes a question about Woman's desire without an object.

If Lilith is the Woman who could not exist, then Eve is the woman who does exist. What I mean by this is that if Lilith is Woman, and the Woman does not exist in the Symbolic because Woman is by her very nature unable to exist fully within the phallic logic, Eve is the woman partially castrated. She is made from Adam's rib, not only meaning that she lacks, but also that he had to give up a piece of himself (the phallus) in order for there to be, not just an other, but for him to exist as well. If Adam was made in the image of God, in order for him to become a person unto himself, he must distance himself from God. In giving up his rib, though castration is never voluntary, there is a question as to whether Adam remains in God's image. In order for there to be subjective distinction between I/Other, castration must occur, but then also denied. With Eve being made from the phallus, she is the symptom of man, meaning her existence is meant to deny castration. As long as there is an Eve made from Adam to which she belongs, Adam's phallus is not gone, just contained safely within Eve as his object a.

As mentioned earlier, Lacan claims that it is a mistake of the masculine subject to believe that the object a lies in another person, as if it was something he could retrieve. Eve then, in being constituted by the phallus and in such constitutes it as belonging to Adam, is always partially under erasure. Being tempted by what knowledge lies outside of the Symbolic displays this quite astutely, as she is not satisfied with what she supposedly has. In fact, Milton may have demonstrated this in *Paradise Lost*, intentionally or not, by having Adam keeping company with the angels, as opposed to Eve, in a seemingly Garden of Eden edition of Fort Da. It is this version of woman that leads Ecclesiasticus (25:24) to claim, "of the woman came the beginning of sin, and through her we all die." I would like to suggest that the use of the term "with" rather than "from" or "because of" allows for an interpretation that may account for a question about the epistemological differences of sexuation. Sin, in this context, is the failure of the sexual relationship. Sin begins with woman, because castration begins with being removed from Woman, and we all perish because her very existence reminds us of such. Her existence is evidence of castration, and in seeking what the Tree of Knowledge may have been able to provide is to refuse to deny it.

Saints and witches

The discourses and knowledge that these myths produced are reiterated in contemporary representations of fallen or evil women. I have also argued that implicit in those portrayals are questions and concerns regarding sexual difference. I would like to turn now to the ways in which those questions of sexual difference could be said to play out on the bodies and experiences of those I am identifying as feminine subjects, or at the very least, subjects who are constituted as such given a specific sociohistorical context. There are two specific examples I would like to examine more closely: saints and witches. I am confining my considerations to saints and witches in the 14th–16th centuries, though I am aware that there are many in the 21st century who identify and practice as witches.

Saints and feminine jouissance

In Seminar XX, while putting forth his ideas regarding feminine jouissance, Lacan explicitly cites mystics as examples of such. For this reason, I will briefly recount his speculations and then offer some further considerations regarding saints and the question of sexual difference, focusing specifically on the public's general orientation to such figures. Lacan (1972) explains that "mysticism is not everything that isn't politics. It is something serious, about which several people inform us" (p. 76). He further explains that though there have been those who have claimed to experience mysticism, their experiences may be better understood as perverse jouissance (jouissance stemming from a perverse subjective structure), such as Angelus Silesius, who takes great pain and pleasure in the experience of being watched by God. Instead, he suggests, the "essential testimony of the mystics consists in saying that they experience it, but know nothing about it" (Lacan, 1975, p. 76). As explained in greater detail earlier, this is to say that whatever feminine jouissance is, it cannot be spoken about because to speak is to derive phallic jouissance. However, Lacan identifies both Hadewijch and Saint Teresa of Ávila as mystics who clearly have a sense of this beyond, suggesting that one only need to see Bernini's statue, "The Ecstasy of St. Teresa" in Rome to immediately understand that she is experiencing orgasm, but it is not clear from where she derives her pleasure. Furthermore, he explains that the writings by these women, what he playfully refers to as "mystical jaculations" (1975, p. 76), are not empty verbiage, but rather concerted attempts to language this jouissance beyond representation.

Lacan refers to, "The Ecstasy of St. Teresa" by Bernini, which depicts a scene Teresa describes in her writings, in which an angel thrusts a flame-tipped arrow into her, leaving her on fire (Buckley, 2014). She remarks,

> It pleased our Lord that I should see the following vision a number of times. I saw an angel near me, on the left side, in bodily form. This I am not wont to see, save very rarely ... In this vision it pleased the Lord that I should see it thus. He was not tall, but short, marvelously beautiful, with a face which shone as though he were one of the highest of the angels, who seem to be all of fire: they must be those whom we call Seraphim ... I saw in his hands a long golden spear, and at the point of the iron there seemed to be a little fire. This I thought that he thrust several times into my heart, and that it penetrated to my entrails. When he drew out the spear he seemed to be drawing them with it, leaving me all on fire with a wondrous love for God. The pain was so great that it caused me to utter several moans; and yet so exceeding sweet is this greatest of pains that it is impossible to desire to be rid of it, or for the soul to be content with less than God.
>
> (Peers, 1927, p. 197)

This sweet pain she describes is what Lacan understands as feminine jouissance, specifically because it has no point of origin and consumes her whole being. This love of God goes beyond the phallic instantiations of the Church, and instead God consumes her, thus making this jouissance beyond any representation in religious ritual or totem.

Before experiencing religious ecstasy, Teresa's relationship to the Catholic church was complicated. As Mujica (2010) explains, Teresa's family, who were Jewish, converted to Catholicism in the early 1500s under the pressure of the crown, and Teresa entered a convent at the age of 14 to avoid a family scandal. Though Teresa did eventually take her vows, Mujica explains further, she also practiced under the teachings of Franciscan Francisco de Osun for twenty years. This practice was grounded in a quiet reflection in order to cultivate an intimate relationship to God, which supposedly led to experiences akin to the description in the paragraph above. Though Teresa of Avila is only one saint of many, her experiences of God tend to be reflected in a number of other writings by mystics. For example, English mystic Margery Kempe (2001) writes of the Lord giving her a flame in her breast that was "wonderfully hot and delectable and right comfortable, not wasting but ever increasing of flame..." (p. 64).

Interesting here, Kempe refers to the fire burning within her, but that which a man would have to reach out and touch, once more reifying the not-whole on the side of woman and the not-all on the side of man.

However, skepticism about a woman's ability to access God without the intervention of clergy led some to investigate. In her work on the origins of human dissection, Park (2006) explains how some of the earliest medical dissections happened in the 13th and 14th century in Italy on the bodies of deceased mystics and the practice arose out of this concern and skepticism. When Chiara of Montefalco died in 1308, the nuns she lived with opened her body to remove her heart with the intention of preserving her body as a sign of respect and tribute to her sanctity. However, when they opened up her heart, they claimed to have seen the image of the crucified Christ in it, along with three stones in her gallbladder, which was assumed to represent the holy trinity (Park, 2006). Park explains that members of the church spoke out about these mystics and argued whether or not they should be recognized as saints. For example, Brother Tommaso di Buono of Foligno, a Franciscan friar, suggested that Chiara's ecstatic states were likely from uterine suffocation. Park goes on to explain that this concern about the legitimacy of female mystics might undermine the ecclesiastical authorities, and further contribute to the move away from religious institutions and to spiritual practices that encouraged asceticism and poverty, which had been attracting many more women than men at the time. This led many to be suspicious about female spiritual leaders, which was aided by the suspicion that women were also more likely to be seduced by the Devil and his demons due to their assumed fragile constitution. Dissection, which was done almost exclusively on women, then provided a means to demonstrate that the mystics were communing with God and not the Devil, as it was common knowledge that God lived in the heart, whereas demons would inhabit the bowels (Park, 2006).

The dissection of female mystics demonstrates an early occurrence of a theme in the discussion of sexual difference. Feminist scholars have emphasized the role of the body and women's oppression, with women being confined to the body and governed by it, whereas men are assumed to be subjects of the mind and rationale, or the need for a consideration of subjectivity beginning from the site of the female body to complement the traditional psychoanalytic preference for the male body (Irigaray, 1985; Braidotti, 2011; de Beauvoir, 2011). From a Lacanian perspective, the female body is constituted by the absence of the phallus, and, therefore, a (partial)lack of a lack. The concerted interest in women's bodies in modernity takes on many forms through the medical establishment and its discourses, but with the mystics in the 14th and 15th centuries, it is clear that the dissection of their bodies was in the hopes of finding something—a presence that would symbolize and thus provide meaning to her ecstatic experiences. It was argued that the images found in Chiara's heart demonstrated that her uterus was ill, further illustrating the tension between making meaning of the woman's body and its ability to evade that meaning. As this tension was confined within the parameters of religious doctrine, it would have been appropriate for this counterargument to index spiritual concerns or assumptions about the Devil's influence, but rather it was her body that was considered the site of suspicion and doubt. This will be demonstrated further when the persecution and prosecution of witches shortly after Chiara's time begins and the woman's body is epitomized as the site of not only sin, but also the vessel through which meaning is ineffectively attempted to be determined.

Witches and the threat of feminine jouissance

Though many of the saints and mystics were stigmatized during their lives, some of whom experienced cruel treatment and were met with dubiety about their experiences, the submission to the paternal Law, in this case the Church, to regulate or determine the meaning of this Other jouissance, allowed them to still participate within society, which in some cases, saved their lives. However, with this comes the implicit assumption that these experiences, and the people who are susceptible to them, are dangerous outside the confines of the Church and its ability to regulate order via its authoritative position within the Symbolic order. It also raises questions about what is unique about these particular people in the first place. Though there was question at the time that the aforementioned mystics were actually heretics, which led to some of them being executed, such as the very famous case of Joan of Arc, it was typically women whose eccentricities were not ensconced, and thus protected by, the Church that were persecuted and tortured for speculations about their involvement in witchcraft … Witchcraft, in contrast to mysticism, in which the women were in communion with God, was understood as consorting with the Devil. Though I believe that a case could be made for considering witches as also being beholden to feminine jouissance, my interest is more so in contrasting their perceived jouissance with that of the mystics in order to consider how the law mediates and sanctions other jouissance.

Considering the fact that the majority of witches persecuted were women, not to mention the discourses pertaining to female sexuality and witchcraft, there is a unique opportunity to investigate the blurred boundaries between fantasy and reality in reference to the sexual relationship. As Skott-Myhre (2015) illustrates, the origin of the term "witch" is difficult to pin down, with it being used to refer to a number of different types of women, including those with the ability to use herbs and potions, not to mention evil spirits, for their own means, as well as to midwives in the Bible and for those who practiced pagan rituals. Though women were not the only victims during the witch hunts, the dissemination of knowledge about the criteria for someone to be considered a witch tended to implicate women first and foremost. It is this dissemination of knowledge that I am particularly interested in for the purposes of this book. Similar to the aforementioned myths and stories, the questions of sexual difference lie at the junction of what can be said and what is unable to be accounted for, and these questions may then give rise to the practices enacted on the body of those identified as having access to a surplus jouissance. There seems to have been a question and concern about sexual difference, and that concern tended to manifest with questions about a woman's relationship to a phallus of some sort, whether it be her husband's or a son of her own.

During the Renaissance, questions about sexual difference seem to have manifested in the attempts to stifle any practices that challenge the authority of the site of knowledge production, in this case, the Church. I will focus specifically on *Malleus Maleficarum*, which translates to "Hammer of the Witches," published in 1487, which provided a detailed legal and theological treatise on the excavation and extermination of witches. Though men were also tried for witchcraft, the 200 years following the publication of *Malleus*, saw between 70–80% of those tried as witches to be women (Broedel, 2003). Broedel explains further that though *Malleus* is quite detailed in the ways in which a witch could be identified and how she should be treated, there is an uninterrogated assumption that a witch is likely to be a woman. He further elaborates that many scholars have explained the practices outlined in the handbook to be symptomatic of misogynistic clergy, clerical practices, and interpretations of Biblical canons that favor antagonistic perceptions of women. For example, Smith (2002) notes that these practices demonstrated a mental or moral pathology of the witch hunters. However, a psychoanalytic lens allows for a consideration of what lies underneath this misogyny or morality, and to question how anxiety and abjection can be said to at work. This is not to sympathize with those who enact harmful, even cruel, practices against women, but rather to try to gain an understanding about the ways in which anxiety about the nonsexual rapport can manifest.

In order to do this, I want to look more closely at the handbook and the discourses therein, rather than speculate about the nature of the individuals writing or reading it. A discursive approach considers the way language constructs identities and relationships without going so far as to assume psychological characteristics. Using discourse analysis along with a psychoanalytic interpretation then asks how jouissance and assumptions about the sexual nonrapport are conveyed via language. There are two distinct depictions of the ways in which witches threaten the perceived sexual rapport that I would like to investigate. First of all, it was suggested that women who were single or childless were the most likely to fall victim to the Devil, likely making a deal with him. In so doing, the job of the witch was to recruit others for the Devil. It was also suggested that women who had befallen hard times were likely to consult the knowledge of a witch or were tempted by the sexual prowess of devils and demons. In fact, a woman was said to become a witch by first having sexual relations with the Devil (Institoris and Sprenger, 2016). The conflation of knowledge and sexual gratification is important here. Institoris and Sprenger go on to use the story of Adam and Eve to demonstrate how women are "more given to the fleshly lusts than a man" and that this is because "she was formed from a curved rib, that is, from a chest-rib, which is bent as it were in the opposite direction from a man" (p. 75). Depictions of witches then tend to emphasize their carnal nature as something in contrast to male sexuality, with illustrations of ecstatic women in orgies with other women, devils, and palpable, incorporeal presences. This is, of course, reminiscent of the ways in which the saints were said to have experienced ecstasy from the lack of a presence. That is, it is the lack itself and not presence, that is, the phallus, which is considered to be the source of feminine jouissance.

Throughout this handbook are stories about the various practices of the witches and how they would enact their magic, some which, as Smith (2002) claims, sound more like bawdy jokes than a legal treatise. These stories include women being led astray by the devil and his demons, even while they slept, and though they did not consciously commit heresy, they were said to have reveled in their sin, witches killing babies while in the womb, and turning people who wrong them into animals. Though all of these stories are rife with potential for theoretical speculations, I will focus on one in particular that has direct implications for a psychoanalytic approach to the questions of sexual difference and abjection. One concern that Institoris and Sprenger return to a number of times is that of men either losing their sexual organ or being "glamoured" or tricked into thinking that they have lost it. Smith (2002) explains that this idea is present throughout *Malleus*, with stories about witches having a nest of homeless male sex organs or by casting spells on young men who can no longer find their implement just as they are about to engage in intercourse. In fact, many of the ways in which the witches intervene tends to be related to disrupting the sexual relationship, and preventing men, in Lacanian terms, offer up what they (do not) have.

The underlying anxiety here is tenable, perhaps too much so to be called unconscious. However, I would like to suggest that the speculations in this text cannot be separated from the occurrence of female mystics at the same time, and that questions about sexual difference which could not be contained by the paternal Law of the Church, manifested in folklore, which subsequently influenced the practices and treatment of anyone suspected of witchcraft. In another story, a young man had become quite depressed because though he wanted to have sexual relations with a young woman, he was unable to "see or touch anything (on himself) except a body that was flat and even" (Institoris and Sprenger, 2016, p. 150). When he converses with this young woman about his situation, it is revealed that it is likely his ex-girlfriend who placed him under a spell. He then waits for his former lover on a road after dark, and when she passes he confronts her. She claims ignorance, but once he begins to strangle her with a towel, she promises to cure him, which she does by touching his thighs and stating, "Now you have what you want" (p. 150) and his phallus is restored to him. A similar story recounts a young man talking to a priest about his missing organ, and when the priest is also unable to see it, he urges the young man to go and confront the woman he believed to have put a spell on him and to "soften her with promises and flattering words" (p. 151).

Latent in these stories is an assumption that there is something about a woman that not only makes her susceptible to consorting with the Devil and his demons, but also gives her the ability to dispossess a man of his phallus. These stories demonstrate an element of fantasy that could not be separated from the practices of torturing and murdering perceived witches. Furthermore, the discourses circulating at the time around women's sensibilities and characters being weaker to withstand outside influences mixed with the religious attitudes of the times, and the cannonification of the mystics as saints, provided enough fodder for rich fantasy material. Rather than suggesting that these attitudes reflect an unconscious desire or question about the nature of sexual difference, I would like to suggest that these stories and practices could perhaps serve as some sort of primal scene from which the modern era works to repress. Modernization and its practices toward women, though assumed to be progress, contains with them traces of these fantasies regarding the desire of woman. I will argue later that this is precisely why Freud and Lacan remain unable to answer the question "What does a woman want?" However, for now, I would like to demonstrate how also present within these fantasies regarding women and their ability to commune with God and the Devil is still a surplus that such explanations cannot account for. I will also argue that this surplus cannot help but extend into modernity along with the aforementioned traces of these somewhat primal scenes, but first I will discuss why this surplus is particularly important in considering political utility of subjectivity and sexual difference.

Encounters with becoming-woman

Unlike the stories about Eve or Medusa, the lives of many saints and mystics have been documented, usually by themselves and tend to be elevated to the level of (auto)biographical accounts, whereas Christian and Greek myths are still commonly referred to as parables. However, though these women wrote about their own experiences, a question regarding sexual difference can still be said to be implicit in these depictions, as from a Lacanian perspective, to speak is to wield the phallus and phallic jouissance. Though these accounts may rely on utilizing symbols and syntax, there is also the explicit disclaimer that what is spoken does not properly account for what was experienced. What this introduces then is that the subject on the side of feminine jouissance, in being a split subject as well, also contains within her a question about this other jouissance that is reliant on the occurrence of sexual difference. If the myths, written by men, convey a certain sense of horror, these accounts by mystics attempt to reconcile that horror with their faith. As Kristeva (1982) suggests, the mystic's relationship with abjection is in infinite jouissance, not in a masochistic sense, but rather in a way that "displaces (abjection) indefinitely [as happens with dreams, for instance] within a discourse where the subject is resorbed [is that grace?] into communication with the Other and with others" (p. 127). Kristeva explains earlier in her work on abjection that, in the bible, rituals focused on the symbolic excision of defilement serve as a means to point to an autonomous force, the Other's jouissance, which threatens divine agency. Divine agency, in this context, should be understood as constituted under paternal Law, which the mystics seemingly transgress, similar to those transgressions of Eve or Medusa, that accesses the Other through abjection as opposed to participating in those symbolic gestures that still allow for subjective space from the Other. The stories and myths then begin as a cautionary tale regarding the fall of man via women, with practices that reinforce that assumption, as is in the case of the persecution of women as witches. However, there lies a tacit suggestion about what is at stake in transgressing the Law, which is then exemplified in the writings of the mystics. It is in this trace in which, I argue, there are implications for thinking through becoming-woman.

It is important to note that mystics and saints communicated their experiences within the confines of the same discourses that perpetuated these cautionary tales. Therefore, in order for them to give an account of themselves, they must construct these experiences by negotiating those discourses that seem to demand a subordination of the feminine. As Kristeva (1982) notes, religious prohibitions in a given society tend to correspond to sexual prohibitions that serve to separate men and women and to ensure the power of the former over the latter. If this assertion is considered psychoanalytically, and women are understood in the ways I have previously laid out, then the mystics in particular provide a unique means for considering the productive possibilities in transgressing the Law through a confrontation with sexual difference in the form of abjection that is best understood as becoming-woman. In his work on becoming-woman in horror films, O'Conor (2010) asserts that the site of becoming-woman has been commonly understood as psychosis but should rather be regarded as the site of creative production. For this reason, I am not as concerned with whether or not the saints were actually communing with God, or if Eve and Medusa were real or not. Instead, I seek to question how their presence can be understood as an embodiment of sexual difference, and how an encounter with this manifestation of difference produces a liminal space in which the creative production inherent in becoming-woman effects a trace in those discourses and practices that attempted to produce knowledge about this Other jouissance. What becomes interesting, then, is what must happen after there is an encounter.

While I argued that this is what elicited certain practices that harmed or killed women, it also effectively subverted any attempts to confine women to this particular instantiation of Woman.

I have argued that these myths and understandings of the lives of the mystics can be understood as a question about sexual difference, and thus a problem that must be solved. Lacan, however, was quite clear about the resolution of this problem—there is not one. This is what he means when he claims that there is no sexual relation. There is no accounting for this surplus jouissance on the side of the feminine subject. However, as Marrati (2006) states in her discussion on Bergson, "a problem defines a field of possible experience, it sets out the meaning of the questions one can ask and prefigures the cases of its solution" (p. 313). If sexual difference is a nonrelation, then attempts to reconcile it via knowledge, will always produce a becoming-woman. That is, if becoming-woman deterritorializes the phallic identities, and confrontation with sexual difference via the abject results in horror or anxiety, which demands a reaction, the subject in question on the feminine side is always pushed to another line of flight in her becoming. Rather than knowing something about "Woman," the knowledge of the given context effaces her own constitution of "Woman." This is seen in the attempts to keep women out of the church, segregating them for spiritual purposes, and of course, burning them at the stake.

Furthermore, Deleuze and Guattari (1980) suggest that an assertion of "Woman" for the purposes of political mobilization can stand as a "molar confrontation" and thus a tactic in a "molecular women's politics" (p. 276). This means, as Colebrook (2000) suggests, that an instantiation of "Woman" then must not simply be in relation to man, whether it be through identification or opposition, but "must affirm itself as an even in the process of becoming" (p. 2). As mentioned earlier, Deleuze and Guattari identify Virginia Woolf as an example of someone "never ceasing to become" (p. 277), and Colebrook (2000) furthers this by suggesting that it is her stream of consciousness style that effects a becoming-woman, as opposed to those writers who express an already-assumed female identity. Colebrook goes on to explain how in taking Woolf as an example, the task for feminism then should not be to only identify wrongs, but to think differently, specifically about the nature of subjectivity, identity, and I will add, sexual difference. It is this thinking differently that allows a political movement to move.

This is where the lives of the saints, as well as the stories recounted here about sphinxes and monsters, effect a change in thinking at the level of the unconscious. Though it may be an oxymoron to discuss thinking and the unconscious together, what I mean to say is that a confrontation with these molar instantiations of "Woman," who cannot help but be more than what is contained in that understanding of the term, cannot help but elicit an unconscious becoming. It is becoming-woman specifically because the encounter via the abject, implicitly questions the status of the phallus, that is, subjectivity as we have come to know it. Responses to that provocation may become varied, such as the aforementioned burning of witches, religious rituals, or even something simple as an assumed moral from a myth or tale inevitably fail, and something else must occur. I want to suggest that this contributes to the change in discourse and practice from attempts to know the soul and spiritual connection with God or the Devil that women had, to attempts to make her body a living cadaver via the medical doctrines of the Enlightenment, which I will turn to in the following chapter. Implicit in these changes is a movement in an attempt to account for that which cannot be accounted for. However, prior to that movement, just following the provoked anxiety, lies a liminal space in which subjectivity as it has been known ceases to exist. This is the horror that lies within sexual difference and the latent potential of becoming-woman in the abject.

References

Braidotti, R. (2011). *Nomadic subjects: Embodiment and sexual difference in contemporary feminist theory*. New York: Columbia University Press.
Broedel, H.P. (2003). *Malleus Maleficarum and the construction of witchcraft: Theology and popular belief*. Manchester: Manchester University Press.
Buckley, F.H. (2014). Men of the Baroque: The sculptor & the poet. *New Criterion, 33*(2), 33–35.
Cixous, H. (1992). *Coming to writing and other essays*. Cambridge: Harvard University Press.
Cohen, D. (2006). *Lilith's ark: Teenage tales of Biblical women*. Philadelphia: The Jewish Publication Society.
Colebrook, C. (2000). Introduction. In I. Buchanan and C. Colebrook (Eds.), *Deleuze and feminist theory* (1–17). Edinburgh: Edinburgh University Press.
Creed, B. (1999). *The monstrous-feminine: Film, feminism and psychoanalysis*. New York: Routledge.
de Beauvoir, S. (2012). *The second sex*. London: Vintage Books.
Deleuze, G. and Guattari, F. (1980). *A thousand plateaus: Capitalism and schizophrenia*. Minneapolis: University of Minnesota Press.
Freud, S. (1922). *Beyond the pleasure principle*. Vienna: International Psychoanalytical.
Freud, S. (2010). Femininity. In L.G. Fiorini and G.A. Sas Rose (Eds.), *On Freud's femininity*. New York: Routledge. (Original work published in 1933).
Hammer, J. (2017). Lilith, lady flying in the darkness. *My Jewish Learning*. Retrieved from www.myjewishlearning.com/article/lilith-lady-flying-in-darkness/
Homer. (1997). *The Illiad*. London: Penguin Classics.
Institoris, H. and Sprenger, J. (2016). *Malleus Maleficarum*. Jazzybee Verlag.
Irigaray, L. (1985). *Speculum of the other woman*. Ithaca: Cornell University Press.
Kempe, M. (2001). *The book of Margery Kempe*. L. Staley (Ed.). New York: W.W. Norton & Company.
Kristeva, J. (1969). *Desire in language: A semiotic approach to literature and art*. New York: Columbia University Press.

Kristeva, J. (1982). *Powers of horror: An essay on abjection.* New York: Columbia University Press.
Kvam, K.E., Schearing, L.S. and Ziegler, V.H. (1999). *Eve and Adam: Jewish, Christian and Muslim readings on Genesis and gender.* Indianapolis: Indiana University Press.
Lacan, J. (1972). *The seminar of Jacques Lacan: On feminine sexuality, the limits of love and knowledge (Encore).* New York: W.W. Norton & Co.
Lacan, J. (1975). Of structure as an inmixing of an otherness prerequisite to any subject whatever. In R. Macksey and E. Donato (Eds.), *The structuralist controversy: The language of criticisms and the sciences of man* (186–200). Baltimore: John Hopkins University Press.
Marrati, P. (2006). Time and affects: Deleuze on gender and sexual difference. *Australian Feminist Studies, 51*(21), 313–325.
Milton, J. (2003). *Paradise lost.* London: Penguin Classics.
Mujica, B. (2010). *Sister Teresa.* New York: Overlook Books.
O'Conor, T. (2010). 'Uncontrollably herself': Deleuze's becoming-woman in the horror films of Michael Almereyda. *Intellect Limited, 1*(1), 111–128.
Ovid. (2014). *Metamorphoses.* London: Penguin Classics.
Park, K. (2006). *Secrets of women: Gender, generation and the origins of human dissection.* New York: Zone Books.
Peers, E.A. (1927). *Studies of the Spanish mystics.* Hampshire, England: The Sheldon Press.
Skott-Myhre, K. (2015). The feminization of labor and the DSM-5. *Annual Review of Critical Psychology, 12*, 71–78.
Smith, M. (2002). The flying phallus and the laughing inquisitor: Penis theft in the Malleus Maleficarum. *Journal of Folklore Research, 39*(1), 85–117.
Sophocles. (1991). *Oedipus Rex.* New York: Dover Publications.
Wilk, S. (2014). *Medusa: Solving the myth of the Gorgon.* Oxford: Oxford University Press.

Chapter 4

Sexual difference and the medical gaze

> The clinic—constantly praised for its empiricism, the modesty of its attention, and the care with which it silently lets things surface to the observing gaze without disturbing them with discourse—owes its real importance to the fact that it is a reorganization in depth, not only of medical discourse, but of the very possibility of a discourse about disease.
>
> (Michel Foucault, *The birth of the clinic*)

In contrast to the Middle Ages, the Enlightenment saw the advent of a biomedical approach to the question of sexual difference. In referring to the Enlightenment, I am more interested in following Foucault's (1966) understanding of epochs, in which historical periods are better conceptualized by the knowledge they produce, as opposed to their calendar years. For example, to talk about the importance of medical discourses as a source of authority during the Enlightenment, should not eclipse the fact that religious discourses still had a great deal of power as well, with the Spanish Inquisition lasting into the 18th century, during the supposed Age of Reason. Moreover, it does not assume that certain practices and approaches had not occurred prior to this era or have remained there. Rather, I would like to consider the ways in which rhetorical devices used during the Enlightenment constructed a notion of a subject premised on sexual difference and how these devices demonstrate evidence of concerns about and defenses against sexual difference. It is during this time in which the medical establishment comes to be understood as the locus of authority regarding the body, and it is through these discourses in which I will now turn to consider the ways in which this anxiety manifests in stories pertaining to monstrous wombs.

The medical gaze and sexual difference

In his work *The birth of the clinic* (1973), philosopher Michel Foucault discussed the ways in which the body became the site of biopolitical medical discourses. He uses the term "medical gaze" to describe the ways in which the body became subjected to the authority of the medical institution and separated from the identity of the person, marking it as a site of political struggle. Under the medical gaze, the body became a source of knowledge for doctors, as opposed to clergy in early eras who were concerned with the soul and were thus the bearers of an otherwise hidden truth.

Foucault also remarked that the advent of the medical authority and its discourses mark an epistemic shift in the production of knowledge. The 18th century ushers in a shift in the ways in which pathology and disease are spoken about; from language reliant on fantasy and imagery to rationalist discourse that assumes objectivity, and thus the totalizing gaze of the doctor. He argued that during the 18th century, words and objects had not yet been separated and it is with the birth of the clinic that the relationship between the visible and the invisible changed, allowing for the gaze and the language founded by it to reveal what had been previously inaccessible. This is not to assume that prior approaches were necessarily naïve or that doctors and technology had improved in such a way that they were able to finally access a previously obscured truth. Rather, doctors trained prior to the 18th century were ensconced in an entirely different practice predicated on an understanding of knowledge as representation, as well as a different relationship between the doctor and the patient. This shift in the production of knowledge subsequently placed doctors and medical authorities as being in the position of the ones who held knowledge in contrast to their patients, who must then be the ones who are in possession of a body about which they do not know.

What I would like to suggest is that prior articulations regarding a woman's soul and sensibilities became inadequate during the Enlightenment because of this adherence to knowledge as representation. The body of the woman as the site of sexual difference became subjected to the medical gaze, which subsequently produced knowledge of sexual difference premised in representation and similitude, which relied on the male body as the site of identification. This follows Deleuze and Guattari's assertion that the male body became a molar instantiation, and thus, used as the locus of corporeal representation, with the female body constantly undergoing change depending on the ways in which it became understood. Thomas Laqueur (1990) writes that prior to the 18th century, the female body was considered an inverted male body, with thinkers such as Galen arguing that women had all of the reproductive parts of men but located internally. This one-sex theory and its considerations reflect observations made in the previous chapter, in which women's bodies and souls were understood as an imperfect version of the male's. Reflected here is the implicit assumption that there is a sexual relation, reminiscent of Aristophanes' hermaphroditic soulmates. With the shift of knowledge being premised in representation and the male body being the standard, the female changes from being an inverted male body to possessing something distinctly different in its own right. Laqueur suggests that this is when the one-sex theory becomes the two-sex theory, and for my purposes, there is a consideration of sexual difference, though still under the assumption that there can be a sexual relation.

I would like to argue here that though medical knowledge relied on representation and that though there was a shift from a one-sex theory to a two-sex theory, concerns regarding the capacities and capabilities of woman as the site of difference manifested in speculations about the female body. These speculations tended to rely on an Imaginary apprehension, in the Lacanian sense, of what a Woman was, and were also seemingly preoccupied with a female phallus, either inverted or in the form of a seemingly foreign presence. For example, folklore about teeth or creatures such as crabs and snakes hiding in the vagina circulated alongside medical literature that elaborated about the power of the woman's body to deform or kill her baby while in utero. In juxtaposing the myths with the practices, a representation of difference posits monstrosity on the side of femininity. Foucault explains that the body is a site of regulatory discourses and that it is the doctor who must reveal the truth to the subject. If this is the case, then the truths revealed about women, particularly in unusual circumstances, serve as a scene in which fantasies or Imaginary material, in the Lacanian sense, about the desires of the Woman find representation in the Symbolic, such as in the cases of maternal impressions in the 18th century, Mary Toft, the rabbit breeder, being the most considered.

Maternal imagination and impressions

During the 19th and early 20th century, there were concerns regarding a mother's supposed ability to mark or deform her fetus through the force of her imagination, referred to as maternal impressions or maternal imagination. In fact, there remains great deal of contemporary scientific research investigating the effects of the in-utero development of fetuses and how the environment of the mother can shape or impede that development. For example, pregnant women are advised to not consume a multitude of foods and beverages, as well advised not to partake in many different activities, even though the research on the effects is not only contradictory but also culturally biased, such as the consumption of certain foods or when bedrest is appropriate. This research tends to be conducted by subjecting the pregnant woman and her fetus to a variety of invasive procedures and tests, which produce results that only trained professionals are qualified to read. Mazzoni (2002) discusses in her book on maternal impressions that the development of ultrasound technology was a way of making the invisible visible, which moved the previously secret knowledge of pregnancy from the mother and midwives, who were also typically mothers, to the medical establishment.

Prior to this, however, this secrecy of pregnancy and the closeness of the mother and fetus produced a great deal of curiosity and anxiety from the medical community and their attempts to establish a certain scientific rigor to issues pertaining to gestation. One issue which made repeated appearances in *The British Medical Journal* throughout the 18ths and 19th centuries was maternal impressions, or maternal imagination. Maternal impressions were believed to be the manifestation of the pregnant woman's desires or sensibilities on the body of the fetus. It was believed that such desires needed to be attended to appropriately, either by medical officials or the father. Mazzoni reveals that such concerns were still prevalent in Italy while her own mother was pregnant, and Italian prenatal literature speaks of the ways in which a mother could mark her fetus with coffee or strawberry colored birth marks if a certain craving was not met. Rather than a simple birthmark, doctors of the 18th and early 19th century believed that maternal impressions could seriously deform or kill the fetus in-utero, making the desire of the mother a public health concern.

The following is a case reported in *The British Medical Journal* in 1867 by Dr. J. Warring-Curran about his patient Mrs. E. The following are the words of Mrs. E. to her doctor six months into her pregnancy,

> I have always enjoyed good health until about three months ago, and date the commencement of my present illness from that time. I was passing through a hay-field when a young man, picking up a frog, threatened to throw it at me. I begged him not to; but he did so, striking me in the face. The shock was so sudden and so great that I felt a particular creeping sensation passing over me, ending in sickness of stomach. I was compelled to sit down, otherwise I should have certainly fallen. From that time to the present, I have been more or less unwell. My appetite is impaired, and I have constant thirst, and desire for cold drinks. Just now, my feelings are most peculiar: I cannot sit in the erect position without feeling nausea; there is a sensation of something swimming, as it were, in my womb, so that I am compelled to constantly lie on my back. I have long thought, but feel now *certain*, that my unborn child will resemble a frog.
>
> (p. 468)

Dr. Warring-Curran goes on to explain that he urged Mrs. E. to not dwell on her fears. However, when she did deliver the baby, it was "a monster, bearing as the head, neck and shoulder went, a striking resemblance to a frog ... which took one or two breaths and happily died" (pp. 468–467). Dr. Warring-Curran offers this story up as an ongoing debate regarding the nature of maternal impressions and the role the mother's imagination has on her developing fetus. Similar tales make their way into the journal over several years, with doctors pleading that maternal impressions be taken seriously in the medical community, using their own peculiar tales as evidence. While there were some doctors who debated the prevalence of maternal impressions and their acceptance within the medical community (*The British Medical Journal*, 1891, 1900), it was largely accepted that the mother's body posed a threat to the developing fetus.

Mary Toft

The story of Mary Toft and its subsequent scandal during the 18th century is an example of the fears and fantasies surrounding the female body. Furthermore, I would like to suggest it is also an illustrative example of the way the mother's body becomes interpolated as the site of the abject, which then becomes adopted and elaborated on in psychoanalytic theory. The concerns surrounding what Mary Toft was or was not capable of demonstrate a certain cautious ambivalence about the female body and its reproductive powers. This is not to say that the cases of maternal impressions are entirely implausible. Psychoanalytic theory has long demonstrated that the mind has a profound effect over the body, with Freud continually demonstrating the relationship between somatic symptoms and the unconscious. My intention here continues to be a concern for the ways the woman is spoken about and how those discourses constitute her as a monstrous subject, implicitly excessive.

The British Gazeteer reports that in the summer of 1726, in Goldalming, England, Mary Toft, pregnant at the time, was weeding in her garden when a rabbit caught her by surprise. She decided to chase the rabbit but was unable to catch it. However, she remarked that it inspired in her such a strong longing that she became ill and eventually miscarried. Her longing for rabbits, however, did not cease, and she began craving them and dreaming about them persistently, but was not able to afford the cost to procure them. A few weeks later she reported being in a great deal of pain, and miscarried once more, but this time it appeared to be "a large lump of flesh" (Harvey, 2015, p. 33). Over the course of the next few weeks, Mary Toft proceeded to continue to give birth to a variety of animal parts, most of which were believed to be from rabbits, though it was later discovered that there was also the fur of a cat stuffed with the spine of an eel (Todd, 1995). As Harvey explains, Toft was attended to by six different physicians, some of whom were affiliated with the Royal Court, and though Harvey maintains that none of them had accused of her of a hoax until she confessed, Todd suggests that Dr. Cyriacus Ahlers confirmed the hoax when he examined the bodies of the delivered rabbits and found hay and corn in the pellets and that the bones had been clearly cut with a sharp tool. Regardless of Dr. Ahlers' confirmations, the general public, and its doctors, were still quite intrigued by the case of Mary Toft, the rabbit breeder.

What is interesting in both Mary Toft's case, as well as Mrs. E's, not to mention several other cases reported during this time, is that there is a conflation of woman's desire with a woman's fear, with both understood as a threat to the development of the infant. According to Lacan (2015), it is also perceived as threatening to the development of the subject, as this anxiety does not stem from a longing for the lost object, in the form of the mother's breast, to return, but rather its imminence. The closeness of the mother's body threatens to undo castration and one will be engulfed by the breast-mother. This anxiety, and I would argue, curiosity about what is excluded in representations of sexual difference, led to suppositions, which found representation in the relationship between the mother and the fetus. While the fetus is in the womb, there is no distinction between her and it, and thus her subjectivity is constituted as pertaining to both herself and something other than her; something which must separate from her and become a subject unto his or her self. The threat, then, is the possibility of this not happening, of the mother marking the infant with her desire in a way that prohibits his or her subjectivity. The maternal breast in this case, is always imminent, always pressing on the subject's corporeality. The fear regarding maternal impressions then is an unconscious anxiety projected onto a concern for the infant, which manifests in the need for an intervention of a paternal metaphor or law that promises a cut from the jouissance of the mother. Without that adequate intervention, the mother's jouissance threatens to consume the child, whether it be his life or his body.

Harvey (2018) re-examines the case of Mary Toft with a consideration of the cultural meaning of such an event as situated within certain socio-economic conditions. While she agrees that the context of the Enlightenment and the pursuit of knowledge as a means to understand and control the natural world are indeed important factors in understanding Mary Toft's case, she argues that the threat of an unruly impoverished class is far more pertinent in this case. Mary Toft and her family were quite poor during a time when her town was undergoing several social and economic divisions and controls, one of which was the attempt to limit the expanding population of the poor. Harvey suggests that Toft's rabbit breeding "exploited the reproductive power of laboring women" (p. 82) and the subsequent attempts to punish her and the conspirators should be understood as a threat to "the very poor and indignant" (p. 82) that threatened the ruling elite's social norms. Though this analysis is certainly apt, I would like to suggest that economic interpretations of social stratification to the exclusion of sexual difference misunderstand the ways in which sexual difference is implicit within economic divisions. The economy and the ways in which it cuts and segregates should be understood as an instantiation of the law that subjects either submit to or are subjected to. The ungovernable poor to whom Toft belonged to are those who have not been yet fully matriculated into the system and are thus the unrepresentable excess that threatens the Symbolic function of the economy as law. This is to say that a Lacanian understanding of sexual difference is essential to the analysis of social and economic stratification, in which the monstrous poor and the monstrous woman are one and the same.

Contemporary monstrous wombs

As I mentioned earlier, this fear of the monstrous womb has not been extinguished, with dietary recommendations and prohibitions being given to pregnant women at large, premised in scientific research. Fears about creating monsters, however, became less substantiated by science and concerns were shifted to theories about teratogens and epigenetics. This shift marks the increasing attempts to medicalize and essentialize human phenomena. The concern about exposing the fetus to harmful substances shifts to a concern about turning on or activating certain genes that were latent within the individual. Kellermann (2013), for example, has illustrated that trauma can be inherited, what he refers to as transgenerational transmission of trauma (TTT), which he demonstrates through studies on individuals who survived the Holocaust, and their children. While such a perspective is invaluable, it also represents the ongoing attempts to reconcile psychoanalytic and attachment theories with modern medicine's hyper-individualization tendencies. Essentially, what TTT seems to attempt to account for is the role of the Other, both in the cultural sense and in relation to the immediate caregiver, in the mind and body of the individual. Latent in such an account suggests a continued concern about the role of the woman's seemingly inability to affect a full mind–body split/castration.

Perhaps these are also some of the issues with the persisting inability to reconcile the camps in the contemporary abortion debates. As I write this, the United States of America is in the midst of a wave of strict, conservative legislations on abortion, with Alabama, Kentucky, Georgia, and Missouri passing varieties of "The heartbeat bill." This bill restricts the woman's ability to have an abortion later than 6 weeks, a time when not many women would even know that they were pregnant, while other variations of the bill will not allow an abortion after conception, even in the cases of rape and incest. Many are concerned that such legislation will mean that women who miscarry or who have a stillborn will be prosecuted for manslaughter or even murder. Without going too much detail about either side's argument, it seems that the central question revolves around whether the fetus is distinct enough from the mother's body to warrant its own rights and freedoms. Those who believe that it does, emphasize the fetus's individual corporality, citing development milestones, such as the heartbeat and nervous system, while those on the pro-choice side emphasize the woman's rights and, important for the discussion here, desires. This situates the abortion debate among a long and tenuous history of the relationship between the desire of the Woman and governing bodies of knowledge and legislation. From this perspective, the sides of the debate are on different epistemological grounds, and thus irreconcilable, unless one side concedes to the rules or logic of the other.

Films and fantasies

With modern medicine predicated on a specific presumption of empiricism, diagnostic literature is no longer the place for explicit fantasies about frog babies or rabbit births and, instead, have been relegated to films as the appropriate arena for the voicing of socially sanctioned fantasies. Films such as Cronenberg's (1979) *The Brood* or Scott's (2012) *Prometheus*, which provide disturbing portrayals of monsters created and born from women, usually after being inseminated by an alien entity. *The Brood*, more so than those films that emphasize alien births, represents a meeting of these tensions circulating in the 19th century with modern psychotherapeutic interventions, which similarly identify the body as the locus of frustrated desire. The film centers around a father, Frank, uncovering a psychotherapist's unusual techniques in the treatment of Nola's, his wife who is institutionalized, mental disturbances amidst a series of brutal murders. The therapist has a technique that allows his patients to manifest their mental and emotional problems on their body, resulting in a variety of symptoms. Nola's manifestations turn out to be monstrous children, who murder anyone who has ever harmed her and whom she was traumatized by.

Many of Cronenberg's films tend to lend themselves to a psychoanalytic interpretation, but *The Brood* is rife with themes about embodiment, symptoms, trauma, and sexual difference. Creed (1993) discusses how this film exemplifies the notion of the abject, with the womb not being contained to the inside, but rather represented as a cancerous growth, which Wood (1983) suggests looks more like an enormous penis than a womb. This suggestion harkens back to earlier assumption that the vagina and womb were an inverted penis. The fact that the inside, penis or womb, is now on the outside, elicits a disgust in Frank, as well as the viewers, that gets at the heart of Kristeva's argument about abjection. It is the thing about the mother's body that makes us recoil in order to ensure a hold on our status as subject. While Wood remarks that it looks like a penis, from a psychoanalytic perspective, we can understand it explicitly as a phallus. That is, it is something present in the mother and belief in the maternal phallus means that there is a lack of a lack and that the subject can no longer off a part for his whole (being). Fantasies pertaining to a maternal phallus tend to rely on a perverse structuration, and in this case, the relationship between the spectator and Nola in the film is best understood as perverse. Similarly, in the cases of maternal impressions, the doctors, and to some extent the general public, posit the mother as possessing something both repulsive and excessive, out of which an intermediary object is produced, rabbits, for example, as a fetishistic object to conceal the maternal phallus.

Though Nola is not the only patient being treated, she is the only one who manifests such disturbing symptoms. In fact, due to the complicated nature of her symptoms, she quickly becomes the therapist's favorite patient, ensuring him fame if he can cure her, reminiscent of the doctors who believed they were discovering monstrous births. The other patients in the film present with various skin abnormalities, but Nola's symptoms are intimately tied to her womanhood. Nola does not only become symptomatic, but rather creates monsters which are intimately tied to the sexual assault she experienced as a child. Rather than regarding this film as only a metaphor for psychotherapy and early childhood trauma, it also demonstrates a concern about the ways in which a woman will impart her trauma to her offspring, thus localizing her body as a threat. Her trauma, which can be reconceptualized here as desire in the Lacanian sense, becomes the thing that needs to be controlled. Rather than a concern for ascertaining or gratifying the desire or needs of the woman, the infant as her object becomes the locus of intervention, once more putting an intermediary object between the doctor/public as subject and the Woman who is believed not to lack.

This is where I would like to return to the notion of trauma and why it is important for talking about sexuation as a encounter with horror. Laplanche and Pontalis (1974) discuss trauma as "an event in the subject's life defined by its intensity, by the subject's incapacity to respond adequately to it, and by the upheaval and long-lasting effects that it brings about in the psychical organization" (p. 465). For Lacan, this occurs when there is a confrontation with the Real that cannot be brought into the Symbolic. The challenge of the analyst then is to work with the analysand to try to adequately represent a kernel of this traumatic Real. However, for the feminine subject, there is always a component of experience that remains in the Real, and thus femininity is always premised on trauma, as is confrontation with it. Cronenberg's film portrays an irreconcilable awareness of difference, and the threat of that difference as not simply destructive in the sense of murdering children, but difference which threatens assumed or common-sense knowledge, which as Cronenberg demonstrates, can only come from beyond the phallus. Characters such as Nola or case studies about maternal impressions reflect this demand to tie this kernel of the Real, in this case feminine jouissance, to a symbol or representation that allows the person or persons the ability to reconcile with it. Given the curiosity and mystery of pregnancy and childbirth, it is no wonder that many of the representations of woman as womb or creator emphasize an unmediated creation. Creed argues that this film demonstrates the infantile fantasy of the phallic mother, who possesses her own phallus, and therefore, lacks nothing. She goes on to suggest that the child-monster becomes a physical manifestation of the mother's desire, similar to Freud's argument that through birth a woman would come to possess a phallus of her own.

I would like to shift this argument slightly to suggest that the horror Nola, as well as Mary Toft and other women from the 19th century, elicit is not just because they birthed monsters symptomatic of their desires, but rather those signifiers, which pointed to what had become known as "Woman," began to lose their hold on the thing signified, demonstrating an ontological crisis. In addition to Creed's considerations, I have been suggesting that what can be seen in these cases is a demand for the intervention of a paternal law as a means to contain the jouissance of the Other as likened to a suspicion regarding feminine jouissance. In confrontation with an other's jouissance, neurotics experience a fear reminiscent of the fear that the Other will demand they sacrifice their castration for the Other's enjoyment. The neurotic navigates this by responding in a way that corresponds to their own subjective structure, whether it be hysteric or obsessional. The obsessional is of particular interest because this is how masculine subjects tend to be structured and it is from this perspective that I am attempting to consider the confrontation with sexual difference, though I have also suggested in this chapter that a perverse symptom can also be said to be occurring in regard to the intermediary infant/rabbit object. The obsessional attempts to mitigate his anxiety by creating knowledge about the Other in order to stifle an unconscious awareness of that desire. This offers insight into the repetitive case studies published in *The British Medical Journal* about the various ways in which women have afflicted their babies while in utero and the pleas the doctors made to take maternal impressions seriously, assuming medical knowledge would shore up this intrusion of anxiety about the Other, or for the purposes here, Woman as Other.

Perhaps it is best to understand the proliferation of medical knowledge that relegates the woman's body as the site of abjection as an obsessional symptom, and films such as Cronenberg's *The Brood* as a perverse symptom, demanding that we all look on in fascination. Cronenberg is one of many directors who have attempted to symbolize the unrepresentable in a way that manipulates this disgust and fascination with the woman/mother's body. Other films such as *Possession*, *The Exorcist*, and *Alien*, not to mention many more, posit the woman's body as confusingly grotesque, sexual, and multiple. Horror films have the unique ability to not only map the correlates of unconscious anxiety, but also provide an arena through which this anxiety can be safely explored. In doing so, the incessant and engrossing repetition alien births, demonic spawn, as in the case of *Rosemary's Baby*, and intergenerational trauma, such as in the film *Hereditary*, which I will discuss further in another chapter, rely on the body of the mother in order to portray what is at the locus of the Other's jouissance, as if the body of the Woman itself is inherently excessive. Cronenberg himself claimed that the main theme in his movies was that the main character, usually a man, is repressed, but that they are not meant to be interpreted as some Cronenbergian hero. He goes on to say that he recognizes this is a projection of himself, a part of himself he is unfamiliar with, that he forces himself to investigate, and then use in his art (Breskin, 1992). It is fair to say that Cronenberg's films are a sublimation of what he discovers during his introspection, however, it is not fair to say that they are entirely idiosyncratic. Films index discourses, which circulate as knowledge about a given phenomenon or group of people. Discourses contain within them a structure of fantasy, which gives rise to various portrayals, and though the images associated with the fantasy may change, there seems to be a shared kernel of anxiety that traverses the individual unconscious. From this perspective, speculations about rabbit births, concerns about development in utero, antichoice narratives that demand the infant be understood as an individual and not an object of the mother, and portrayals of alien births all become the symptoms of the sexual difference and the anxiety about the sexual nonrapport that find their manifestations in the appropriate cultural discourses.

It is true that though the unconscious is personal, and the benefit of analysis is best exemplified in a clinical setting, Freud himself relied on myth and story to say something about what he was encountering with his analysands, and similarly these films, alongside the cases of the doctors in the 18th century, provide a screen on which these unconscious anxieties can be articulated through other myths and stories. Braidotti (2011) argues that discourses on monsters in particular tend to be an intersection between the scientific and the fantasmatic, with the imagination being implicated in scientific rationality. Furthermore, as Hook (2017) suggests, jouissance is best understood, not as somehow floating about the Symbolic, but rather intimately tied to it. He argues that jouissance is inherently a social and political factor, as it not only occurs within the Symbolic, but also implies a dialectic of possession, includes the functioning of the law and the superego, and is structured by a certain fantasy about how the other enjoys. Hook applies this understanding of jouissance to instances of racism, as does George (2016). In those moments when woman cannot be fully accounted for by the Symbolic order, when the male/medical gaze must rely on its structured fantasy to apprehend the circumstances, jouissance becomes politicized. It is the potential in this politicized jouissance that I will turn to next.

Becoming-woman and becoming-multiple

These particular encounters with the female body, whether they be during pregnancy and childbirth, or on film in which the former are represented, are indicative of the ways in which women have been reduced to a body part or parts, which have then been studied, sexualized, objectified, and commodified. Recently, attention has been drawn to common representations of the female body as a series of partial objects, such as the ways in which advertising cuts women's heads off and accentuates her breasts and/or buttocks (Leiffreing, 2016). de Beauvoir (2012) argued that women are commonly considered to inhabit the body, while men occupy the mind, which leads many to assume that women are more subject to biology and the shifting tides of nature. However, by considering these representations of women as womb through abjection and jouissance, the nature of the body is already put into question. In emphasizing certain body parts, whether it be those used for reproduction, or those which elicit desire, the spectator is no longer dealing with jouissance, but with the phallus, a part that can be a stand in for the whole and which constitutes his or her desire, that he or she can answer with his or her own phallus to defend against jouissance.

If turning Woman into a constellation of partial objects defends against jouissance, then a consideration of what the opposite configuration might look like may provide an opportunity to discuss the ways in which these representations also challenge conventional, essentialist notions of Woman. If these practices are effective in portraying Woman as a Frankenstein of partial objects, organs without a body, then perhaps considering these women and their monstrous wombs as Bodies without Organs (BwO) can provide a point of departure from phallocentric modes of being. Deleuze and Guattari (1980) state,

> The body without organs is not a dead body but a living body all the more alive and teeming once it has blown apart the organism and its organization ... The full body without organs is a body populated by multiplicities.
>
> (p. 30)

The ways in which the pregnant woman are multiple are perhaps quite obvious, maybe even more so in the case of Mary Toft and her seventeen rabbits. However, if the assumed nature of the body as a static and stable entity is challenged in favor of the BwO, then the rabbits, the frogs, the doctors' concerns, and the various cravings the woman experiences while pregnant are included and become an assemblage with the woman. If what she creates is a monster, then it is important to note that a monster is always, as Braidotti suggests, "the bodily incarnation of difference" (p. 216). Furthermore, Canguilhem (1966) argues that the normal human body is constituted as zero-degree of monstrosity. For Lacan, this zero-degree monstrosity correlates to the degree to which the subject can be represented, with the bodily incarnation of difference being premised on absence. The monster, because it is predicated in difference, will always elicit, demand even, a response from the Other that cannot be predetermined, such as "When I see X, I will do Y."

Molecular (un)consciousnessness and monstrous offspring

Returning to Deleuze and Guattari's appreciation of Virginia Woolf's stream of consciousness, the women in these maternal impression cases were also in a similar state, with the body and bodies being the production and reproduction of consciousness. Also, their bodies were undergoing constant change as they interacted with not only their environment, but also their own partial objects, which also effected doctors, townspeople, their families, etc., in a way that demanded a new response to their assumed container: as Woman. They demanded a production of a new knowledge, and though that knowledge itself tried to hold or pin down the phenomena, it was the act of creation that is interesting for thinking through the potential of these occurrences. Also, in considering this as a stream of consciousness via the BwO, it makes sense that traces and filaments of the questions produced in reaction have found their way into modern cinematic representations when the contemporary moment supposedly favors rationalistic and empirical discourse. With the BwO not being localized in time, but rather having the ability to make up the past, present, and future, these films can be regarded not only as sublimated anxiety of difference, but also as monstrous births themselves, spawning other monstrous-children with other directors, artists, and spectators.

In fact, it is almost impossible to trace the actual lines of flight that something like the case of Mary Toft would have produced, with its decidedly unusual experimentation with the public's imagination about what the female body could do. Following Spinoza, Deleuze (1990) also asks for innovation for thinking through the potential of the human body, not from the perspective of asking what it is, but rather what can it do. Though Mary Toft's case was considered a hoax, for all intents and purposes, she did give birth to rabbits, in that her uterus contracted and rabbit parts were expelled through her birth canal. Similarly, the doctors speculating about cases in the medical journals also seem to be questioning what it is that the body is capable of, and though it may be unconscious anxiety about difference that both demands and attempts to answer this question, the space in between this question and answer exposes the interminable nature of bodies. As mentioned before, the woman's body is more susceptible to this sort of effect, as not only does it confront one with its multiplicity while pregnant, but the woman's body is less overdetermined than man's due to man's need to deny castration. However, this poses its own ethical problems. Though becoming-woman offers opportunities for molecular modes of becoming, the actual lived bodies of the women are still the victim of not only potentially harmful and disembodying medical discourses that scar, maim, and even kill.

Similar to the ways in which the mystics may have affected a trace of sexual difference in the spectator or reader, both the actual encounters between the women and doctor, as well as the representations in medical texts or films, may have produced an affect that could not be contained within medical discourse. If horror movies like *The Brood* reliably demonstrate anything over and over again, it is how disturbing it is to contemporary subjects when science fails to understand or account for certain phenomena. I have suggested that when confronted with the jouissance of the Other, that jouissance is beyond the phallus and threatens subjectivity. This is then responded to by attempts to represent it via some sort of paternal metaphor, whether it be the medical gaze of doctors, or the internalized medical gaze of contemporary Western subjects, which identify a character such as Nola as falling outside the confines of a medical diagnosis. However, this very threat to subjectivity allows for a consideration of the pregnant female body as having the potential to open onto a Body without Organs, in as such as it seems to contain within it a multiplicity and permeable to the environment. Freudian psychoanalysis became one of the more successful tools in explicating something about this relationship to the Other, as well as a consideration of the body as made up of splits and vertices. However, when it comes to the nature of sexual difference, Freud also came up against an impasse regarding the desire of Woman. In the next chapter, I will go deeper into what Freud said about women and how this too was challenged by a particular version of the monstrous-feminine, the mother monster.

References

(1891). Maternal impressions. *The British Medical Journal*, 2(1616), 1322.
(1900). Maternal impressions. *The British Medical Journal*, 1(2036), 37–38.
Braidotti, R. (2011). *Nomadic subjects: Embodiment and sexual difference in contemporary feminist theory.* New York: Columbia University Press.
Breskin, D. (1992, February). Cronenberg: The Rolling Stone interview. *Rolling Stone*, 623(6), 66–70.
Canguilhem, G. (1966). *The normal and the pathological.* New York: Zone Books.
Creed, B. (1999). *The monstrous-feminine: Film, feminism and psychoanalysis.* New York: Routledge.
Cronenberg, D. Director. (1979). *The Brood* [Film]. Canadian Film Development Corporation.
de Beauvoir, S. (2012). *The second sex.* London: Vintage Books.
Deleuze, G. (1990). *The logic of sense.* New York: Columbia University Press.
Deleuze, G. and Guattari, F. (1980). *A thousand plateaus: Capitalism and schizophrenia.* Minneapolis: University of Minnesota Press.
Foucault, M. (1966). *The order of things.* New York: Pantheon Books.
Foucault, M. (1973). *The birth of the clinic.* New York: Pantheon books.
George, S. (2016). *Trauma and race: A Lacanian study of african american racial identity.* Waco, TX: Baylor University Press.
Harvey, K. (2015). What Mary Toft felt: Women's voices, pain, power and the body. *History Workshop Journal*, 80(1), 33–51.
Harvey, K. (2018). Rabbits, whigs and hunters: Women and protest in Mary Toft's monstrous births of 1726. *Past & Present*, 238(1), 43–83.
Heroux, C. and Cronenberg, D. (1979). *The brood [Motion picture].* Montreal, Canada: Canadian Film Development Corporation.
Hook, D. (2017). What is "enjoyment as a political factor?". *Political Psychology*, 4(38), 605–620.
Kellermann, N.P. (2013). Epigenetic transmission of Holocaust trauma. *The Israel Journal of Psychiatry and Related Sciences*, 50(1), 33–39.
Lacan, J. (2015). *On the names of the father.* Cambridge: Polity.
Lacquer, T. (1990). *Making sex: From the Greeks to Freud.* Cambridge: Harvard University Press.

Laplanche, J. and Pontalis, J.B. (1974). *The language of psychoanalysis.* New York: W.W. Norton & Co.
Leiffreing, I. (2016, June 6). The headless women of advertising. *Campaign.* Retrieved from www.campaignlive.com/article/headless-women-advertising/1397529
Mazzoni, C. (2002). *Maternal impressions: Pregnancy and childbirth in literature and theory.* Ithaca: Cornell University Press.
Scott, R. Director. (2012). *Prometheus* [Film]. 20th Century Fox.
Todd, D. (1995). *Imagining monsters: Miscreations of the self in eighteenth-century England.* Chicago: The University of Chicago Press.
Wood, R. (1983). Cronenberg: A dissenting view. In P. Handling (Ed.), *The shape of rage: The films of David Cronenberg* (115–135). Toronto: General.

Chapter 5

Psychoanalysis and the mother-monster

> The great question that has never been answered and which I have not yet been able to answer, despite my 30 years of research into the feminine soul, is: 'What does a woman want?'
> (Sigmund Freud, Letter to Princess Bonaparte)

Lacan's conception of sexual difference, and the issues addressed in this book, arise from Freud's question regarding the desire of woman. This takes seriously Freud's assertion that the job of psychoanalysis is not to answer questions but to open a question that has the potential to shift the subject's ways of relating to herself and others in radical ways. It is no secret that Freud's theories about what constitutes a Woman are problematic, and Soler (2003) notes that these critiques came from his own camp and not just in the following feminist movements. His conceptualizations, however, are important, as are the protests they spurred. For my purposes here, I want to consider how Freud's understanding of feminine desire produced changes in the production of knowledge about the Woman, which also then dictated the correlates for where that knowledge would fail, as well as an encounter with the abject.

Lacan returns to Freud's question about the nature of the women's desire before proclaiming that nothing can be said about it. He then, however, utilizes the figure of the mother and the jouissance of the other to elucidate his understanding of the development of psychoses in the subject. This, however, tends to overlook the actual desire of the mother and instead favors the experience of what the mother must desire. The site of sexual difference then shifts from the mother's body during pregnancy to the mother in relation to her child. While doctors of the 19th century sought intervention in order to protect the child from corporeal disfigurement or death caused by the desire of the mother, psychoanalysis introduces the threat to the subject and his or her unconscious in relation to the mother's enjoyment. This threat heightens in the early 2000s with the series of maternal filicides. I would like to suggest that it is in these cases, specifically the horror elicited in these cases, that the knowledge produced by psychoanalysis about women failed to account for the Woman once more, and where Lacan's theory of the jouissance beyond the phallus could be said to manifest in a more violent way than that of the mystics. Though I do not want to romanticize the suffering these women experienced or inflicted, I am interested in the way they also demonstrated a moment in which they refused subjectivization, demonstrating the sometimes disturbing and disruptive ways in which becoming-woman may manifest. Subsequent reactions and attempts to rationalize and justify the actions then can be seen as a reterritorialization technique on the part of the state apparatus in conjunction with the psychiatric-medical model.

The woman in psychoanalysis

It is important to note that Freud does not put forth a theory as to what a woman is, but rather how a woman comes into being. This distinction is crucial because it already emphasizes the role of early experiences as opposed to any sort of biological essentialism. In fact, Freud's lecture on femininity is conceived of as a riddle since he finds it inadequate to explain the difference between masculinity and femininity in regard to anatomy. Furthermore, in following Felman (1993), the question about what a woman wants emphasizes a radical shift in traditional patriarchal modes of questioning about women. Freud came up against an impasse in his science, and in posing the question, "What does a woman want?" he exposed the problems that both psychoanalysis and society face in regard to knowing something about woman, and in posing it, he subtly suggests that what she may desire has not been what has been prescribed.

Freud (2010) attempted to address the question of sexuality in three distinct ways, none of which account for a feminine essence or sexuality. The first consideration Freud makes is in relation to the drives. For Freud, the drives in the unconscious are always partial, none of which are genital, but rather are sublimated into a desire for genital satisfaction, making all sexuality as a genital organization masculine because of its reliance on the presence of the genitals. As far as the "active" characteristics that are typically associated with the male sex drive, Freud remarks that he sees those traits in both the sexes and is therefore not sufficient of a cause to delineate the difference between the two. The second way in which Freud attempts to organize the sexes is in relation to the penis, which Lacan reconceives of as the phallus via the signifier. For Freud, feminine sexuality is constituted by not having the phallus, whereas masculinity is by the fear of losing it. Soler explains that this idea of the castration complex is a crucial factor in becoming either a man or a woman, which means that it is not the anatomy, but rather the anxiety in relation to the anatomy or the lack thereof, which orients a subject. It is in the discourses of gender performance that the castration complex is most obvious, with masculine roles emphasizing what they have to offer to satisfy the other's incapability, and feminine gender roles concerned with lacking in some way. Finally, Freud conceived of the sexes differently in relation to their object choice for a sexual relation. In this stage of sexual development, that the girl becomes a woman when she comes to expect the phallus, which begins with a desire for a husband and culminates in giving birth to a baby, preferably a male baby, where she will have a phallus of her own.

The mother-monster of the unconscious

Psychoanalysis thus contributes to the notion of the monstrous mother in two ways: the mother as castrated as posited by Freud, and the maternal phallus as demonstrated through the jouissance of the Other. The castrated mother evokes fear, according to Freud, because of her dismembered state. The case of Little Hans exemplifies this, in which Freud argues that Hans' fear of being bitten by a horse stems from castration anxiety and traces it to an early warning from his mother that if he does not stop playing with his "widdler" that a doctor would come and take it off. Though it is the mother who threatens this, it is a doctor who will do the castrating. The mother is monstrous in this regard because she lacks and this realization is considered a developmental milestone according to Freud. Identifying the mother as a deformed is the first instantiation of woman as monster, but it a pathetic monster, one which elicits sympathy along with disgust. Creed, in her critique of Freud and Lacan, suggests that they ignore the fact that many children express fear that it is the mother that tends to utter the castration threat, as in the case of Little Hans, as well as in Freud's famous case of the Wolf Man. She references stories about vagina dentata and cultural myths that portray women's genitals as maiming male genitalia to support her assertions. Though this perspective attempts to place woman in a more active role, one which could be construed as empowering in some way, it still places woman in the position as monster, and more importantly, still in relation to the literal phallus as the site of her constitution.

In moving from the literal phallus to the signification of the phallus, Lacan also positions motherhood in a different way and is one of the first psychoanalysts since Freud who returns to the question regarding women's desire as distinct from motherhood, that is, her desire lies outside of it. Lacan's propositions go beyond the Freudian Oedipus complex, and while the mother is first situated as first attached to the paternal metaphor, she becomes the barred Other, the Other who is not entirely occupied with either the father (paternal metaphor) or the child (the object). The issue according to Lacan, however, is still the relationship between the mother and child, and it is still the male child that is in the most danger. The mother, as Soler argues, or better stated, the person in the maternal function, is the first person to speak the child into being. In being the one who polices the body, whether it be to encourage or scold, she is the one who marks the child with language. This becomes an issue for the child when he or she is caught in the demands of the mother, whether they be domineering or more whimsical. If the mother is the child's first other, and in the position of the Other, then his or her experience of the mother, as opposed the actual desire of the mother as stated above, is to first be the object of the mother, and thus subjected to what is perceived to be her insatiable demands.

The Lacanian mother-monster then is the mother of the unconscious in the place of the Other, which structures the subjective development of her child. As mentioned earlier, the neurotically structured individual responds to the Other by offering up a piece of themselves, usually through language, as a substitute object instead of their whole being as object. In order to do this, however, there needs to be a paternal metaphor that effects a separation between mother and child/object. Lacan (2015) emphasizes that this paternal metaphor does not need to be the literal father, suggesting that one could do without the (literal) father, provided he is used (paternal metaphor or the Law). In using it, the mother as Other, or m(O)ther, hints at something about her desire, specifically that it lies elsewhere. Soler demonstrates that she can do this in several ways, such as "through her contradictions, her silences, her gaps, her equivocations- everything she does not say of her desire but that she allows the young subject's eager ears to hear" (p. 119). However, a problem arises when there is no limit to the mother's love for her child/object, and when its existence is predicated on being her object. When this occurs, castration cannot affect subjectification and Lacan argues that the child is at risk of being psychotically structured. If the neurotic structure is constituted by lack, the psychotic structure is constituted by a lack of lack. The person in the psychotic position experiences no separation from the Other and is thus victim to the jouissance of the Other.

It is in Lacan's conception of psychopathology that sexual difference is once again at the forefront of unconscious concerns. Critics such as Luce Irigaray, Héléne Cixous, Bracha Ettinger, Julia Kristeva, and Judith Butler have commented on Lacan's inability to challenge the phallocentrism of Freud and therefore positions the mother as the cause of suffering to the exclusion of other profitable insights. In his defense, what Lacan offers that other theories of difference do not necessarily, is a consideration of how a question about the Other, and thus sexual difference, can inform behaviors and ideas, questions which were presented to him by his analysands. A question offers room for considering both the ways in which the subject fills in the answer himself or herself how these answers could be shifted, as well as space to speculate about the anxiety latent in the question. However, in theorizing what is revealed to him during analysis, Lacan too takes part in positioning the mother as the site of sexual difference and the anxiety that that produces. This anxiety is then reformulated through a subjective structure that dictates the subject's engagement with the m(O)ther. Finally, I will demonstrate how psychoanalytic, though not necessarily Lacanian, considerations of pathology become implicit in certain contemporary clinical diagnoses, which also struggle with the question of the woman's desire and the status of the subject in relation to her and maintain that the etiology of the disorder lies on the side of the mother, with the paternal metaphor functioning as the adequate or inadequate intervention.

Lacan's understanding of psychic suffering differs from the contemporary biomedical model. Rather, he suggests that subjects are shaped by an unconscious structure, which like most psychoanalytic theories, is formed in relation to early childhood experiences, which are retroactively interpreted through this unconscious structure. According to Lacan, there are two types of neurotic structures, as well as the psychotic and perverse structures that are outside of neurosis. Each structure is characterized by a different relationship to the Other, a different response to the demands of the Other and a difference in the relationship to the return of the repressed (Fink, 1999). It is important to note that the subjective structures are determined by the specific ways that the paternal metaphor frustrates the subject's desires, which will be illustrated later in a discussion on contemporary horror films. For Lacan, what is repressed is not perceptions, but rather this primal desire that is attached to affect. The repressed returns because it becomes associated with seemingly unrelated thoughts and then finds a means to be expressed in dreams, slips of the tongue, and symptoms (Fink, 1996). The return of the repressed manifests according to the neurotic structure of the subject, meaning that the symptoms will speak in a discourse that is very close to the repressed anxieties pertaining to the primal fantasy.

Lacan uses his neurotic structures to then formulate discursive positions, specifically in regard to the hysteric's position. Lacan's reconfiguration of the hysteric into the discourse of the hysteric harkens back to Freud's case of Dora and becomes the original neurotic subject (Gherovici, 2014). The discourse of the hysteric is similar to Freud's in that it is expressed at the level of the body in conversion symptoms. However, as mentioned earlier, Lacan is interested in a structural conceptualization of the discourse of the hysteric as related to the fundamental fantasy, and thus extending Freud's work. Fink (1999) makes a case for referring to the hysteric as a "she" because the majority of individuals in the hysteric position are women. I will follow his lead here, but would like to add that this may be the case because women are frequently the ones to be hystericized by societal discourses that perpetuates woman as hysteric. For the hysteric subject position, the primal fantasy, whereby she comes to recognize the primary caregiver as lacking something, is understood as she is the thing which the Other lacks. She senses that her primary caregiver is incomplete without her, and therefore relates to the Other's lack, as opposed to her own. It is in this apprehension that she understands herself to be the phallus, as opposed to desiring one. However, when during the Oedipus complex, the young girl comes to identify with her mother, or the caregiver who is lacking, she is confronted with the fact that she does not have the phallus, while simultaneously believing herself to be the phallus. It is this conflict that produces the question "Am I man or woman?" that Lacan argues is the essential question that is foundational to the hysteric structure (Lacan, 2019).

While the other neurotic structures are driven by a question as well, it is only in the hysteric's position in which there is a dialogue with the Other. Gherovici (2014) explains that desire for the hysteric is the desire of the Other, and that the hysteric in fact invents the Other and devotedly believes in the Other's existence. It is to the Other that the hysteric asks, "Am I man or woman?" and identifies with whatever answer is provided. However, the answer "You are this ..." then becomes a finite object that can never replace the original lost object. As Gherovici (2014) explains further that because no answer can satisfy the hysterics desire, "the only true answer is no answer at all—silence" (p. 58). This frustration, and suggested solution, becomes paradoxical when psychoanalytic approaches and the role of the quiet analyst is exchanged for contemporary approaches grounded in symptomology, practitioners situated as the source of knowledge, and diagnostic categories imbued with societal discourses regarding normalcy, desirable subjects, and the sources of suffering.

In contrast to the hysteric, the obsessional structure is constituted by a negation of the Other. While most women could be said to be in the hysteric's position, men are over-represented in obsessional neurosis. The obsessive's structure is also related to a lost object in relation to the primary fantasy, but as Fink (1999) explains, "the obsessive refuses to recognize that this object is related to the Other" (p. 118). Rather, the object a is believed to be located within the obsessive, even though it is not. Just as the hysteric experiences the sense of loss when the breast, the primary source of satisfaction, is taken, the obsessional compensates for this by constituting himself in relation to the breast, as opposed to the Other who possesses the breast, as in the case of the hysteric. If this is the fundamental fantasy for the obsessive, he will be compelled to neutralize or destroy the Other, specifically the desire of the Other, that questions his assumptions and exposes his own lack (Fink, 1996). The question that the obsessive formulates in relation to the fundamental question "What am I?" is "Am I dead or alive?" as Fink (1999) explains, "the obsessive is convinced that he is, that he exists, only when he is consciously thinking" (p. 122).

This reliance on the conscious experience places the obsessive in the position of needing to negate the unconscious. He perceives himself to be a complete subject, as opposed to the barred subject that Lacan claimed every speaking subject was. Therefore, it is crucial for the obsessive to negate the desire of the Other, because it puts him in the vulnerable position of confronting the unconscious. Because of this, desire is impossible in this position, because approaching the cause of his desire is to come into direct confrontation with the Other, which subsequently threatens him with his own effacement. As Lacan (1998) states,

> ... the subject appears first in the Other, in so far as the first signifier, the unary signifier, emerges in the field of the Other and represents the subject for another signifier, which other signifier has as its effect the aphanisis of the subject. Hence, the division of the subject- when the subject appears somewhere as meaning, he is manifested elsewhere as 'fading', as disappearance. There is, then, one might say, a matter of life and death between the unary signifier and the subject, qua binary signifier, cause of his disappearance.
>
> (p. 218)

In contrast to hysteria and obsessional neurosis, is psychosis and perversion, which Lacan situated as outside of neurosis because they were characterized differently in relation to the Other. Beginning with psychosis, the mechanism that orients the subject is foreclosure, as opposed to repression in the case of neurosis. This foreclosure is in regard to the paternal metaphor, meaning that the function of the father was not properly utilized and that the cut from the jouissance of the mother was never established in order for the infant to become a subject. As Fink (1999) explains, the role of the father is to thwart the child's attempt to remain one with the mother and to forbid the mother from reaping certain satisfactions from her child. If the hysteric is the cause of the Other's desire and the obsessional negates the desire of the Other, the psychotically structured subject can get no separation from the Other and is constituted by the Other's enjoyment. This is similar to feminine sexuation, except that the feminine subject has a grounding in the Symbolic that allows her to orient herself and experience phallic jouissance. Finally, in regard to language, the neurotic experiences himself or herself coming to be in language, though still alienated, but has the experience of having a familiarity with language, whereas for the person psychotically structured, language is always experienced as outside the subject (Fink, 1999). While the neurotic is alienated in language, the psychotic is possessed by it. In regard to the registers, the neurotic supplants the Imaginary with the Symbolic, whereas for the psychotic, this does not occur. What this means then is that the psychotically structured person does not develop a successful ego-ideal, which allows him to have a sense of who he is in language, and he is dominated by imaginary relations characterized by rivalry and aggression, as opposed to symbolic concerns, such as ideals, authority, rules, achievement, etc. (Fink, 1999).

Finally, perversion is similar to psychosis in that it relies on a failure of the father function, though rather than being constituted by foreclosure, the perverse subject is oriented by a disavowal of the paternal metaphor. Lacan explains that perversion relies on an attempt to evoke the law or bring the law, being the paternal metaphor, into being, as a means to limit jouissance. In regard to the mother, the perverse subject believes that he lacks, but will not accept his own castration. In order to bring the law into being, while simultaneously denying castration, the perverse subject requires that the phallus be veiled, and thus offers up himself or an intermediary object as the object of the Other's enjoyment (Fink, 1999).

In each of these formulations, the subject is attempting to navigate the m(O)ther. At best, the subject can hope to adequately reject the mother and be pleasantly displeased with being cut off from her, but psychologically better for it. Though Lacan and subsequent Lacanian analysts emphasize the failure of the paternal metaphor or father function, it is the ability of the paternal metaphor to protect against the mother that is being evaluated. The mother in the place of the Other is the one who is the cause of frustration, at best, and subjective annihilation, at worst. This characterization of mother as monster aligns closely with Freud's idea that the infant is the mother's phallus; however, it goes a step further and emphasizes a consuming nature of the mother. The threat of the m(O)ther without a paternal metaphor to limit her enjoyment of her child challenges Creed's consideration of the feminine monster as the monster who castrates, and instead is the one who threatens to prevent castration. The experience of anxiety manifests in direct confrontation with the desire, or lack thereof, of the mother. Anxiety, for the neurotic, appears when there is a confrontation with the Real, that is, when lack fails to exist, meaning when the mother's jouissance is too present (Lacan, 2016). In contrast, for the psychotically structured person, the Real is unable to be repressed, so rather than experiencing anxiety in moments of encountering the Real, anxiety is the foundational experience, meaning that the desire of the Other is always imminent.

Mother-monsters in film

This mother-monster makes its way outside of the clinic and into the cultural imagination through film in a way that is slightly different than the aforementioned monstrous uteruses. Modern representations of this type of monster in horror films tend to emphasize a supernatural creature which threatens to take over, absorb, or consume the person, as opposed to the traditional slasher flick that focuses on a more phallic monster with his various blades. Films such as *Possession* (1981), *It Follows* (2014), *The Ring* (2002), and *The Grudge* (2004) demonstrate this sort of monster, in which a young woman is either taken over or terrorized with an ambivalent presence that cannot be satisfied. The threat of the Other's jouissance is probably most clearly depicted in the film *It Follows* (2014). In this film, people pass on a sexually transmitted presence that then stalks them, slowly walking, until it catches up with them and kills them, unless they are able to pass it on to someone else. This presence can take on any persona, and usually blends in with the environment, though only the person it is stalking can see it. Once it catches up to the person, not only does it kill the person, but also it contorts their bodies so that the corpses are not readily identifiable as human bodies. Though this is not a mother figure, though it can take the shape of one's mother, it clearly depicts the anxiety elicited by the Other's jouissance: an omnipresent, encroaching force, that seems to want for nothing other than to consume, the effect of which is the complete loss of bodily unification.

There also seems to be a genre of horror emerging that deals directly with a literal unmoored mother. These films all share the unifying theme of maternal grief. Films such as *Hereditary* (2018), *The Witch* (2015), *Antichrist* (2009), and *The Babadook* (2014) all center around the profound repercussions of the loss of a child. The horror, however, is not the ways in which the death occurs, though also horrifying, but the unleased jouissance of the m(O)ther. These films go beyond the traditional jump scares and instead play with the audience's desperate attempts to hold on to a fixed reality of the film. The result then is not the horrified satisfaction in seeing the dismembered bodies in *Saw* or an adrenaline high anticipating the clever ways in which Michael or Jason maim and murder their victims, but rather, disgusted and bereft without much of a resolution and no alleviation from the suffering that was endured. I do not have the space to go into a synopsis of each film, nor would a synopsis do any of these films justice. For my purposes here, I will refer to *Hereditary* and *Antichrist* as they follow similar trajectories and explore perhaps what Aronson (2019) referred to as a "psychoanalytic conspiracy theory" about sexual difference.

One way of considering these films is as a symptom of the socius. As I will argue more substantially in the next chapter, there seems to be an ongoing concern with a weakening of the paternal function in contemporary society. This is reflected in protests against various identity and sexual politics, within online communities such as Reddit, and even among Lacanians, specifically in the Millerian camp who are suggesting there may be more cases of Ordinary Psychoses, meaning psychotic subjective structures with a functional delusional metaphor, which is predicated on an absent or weak paternal cut. I am not suggesting that there is a weakening of the paternal function, but rather there seems to be a question as to such or what it might mean for it to be the case. These films can then be regarded as a complaint about the sexual non-rapport and a concern about the jouissance of the Other during a political climate that seeks to dethrone the phallus as the site of subjective development. Horror movies have a history of evoking or engaging the law in some way, as I earlier suggested in the works of Barbara Creed and Carol Clover. The movies I am referring to here, however, seem to articulate a nostalgic complaint for a law that once was; a father who would not have let "it" have happened this way.

For a better understanding of this complaint, I turn to Ari Aster's 2017 family horror film *Hereditary*. The film is about a family following the death of Annie's mother, the mother played by Toni Collette. Annie is a miniature artist and many of the scenes or plot points of the film are either illustrated or replicated in miniature scenes, such as when Annie is at group therapy and telling the story of her own mother breastfeeding her daughter, which the audience sees represented in miniature form. The family is coping with the death of the grandmother in their own ways. Paul, the father, attempts to work behind the scenes and do damage control when issues arise, such as when the grandmother's body goes missing. Peter, the teenage son, is the typical melancholic teenager, interested in partying and smoking weed, while Charlie, the eccentric teenage daughter with a tic that manifests as a tongue clicking, seems to also be interested in making miniatures, though more abstract and disturbing than her mother's, as well as decapitating birds. Finally, Annie turns to group therapy where she meets Joan, a woman who lost her grandson and participates in occult practices in order to communicate with him. Though the film begins with a general unease and tension, the true horror occurs when Peter is forced to take Charlie to a party, where she consumes nuts, to which she is allergic. She goes into anaphylactic shock and Peter attempts to rush her to the hospital while she sticks her head out of the window, gasping for air. Peter is forced to swerve when an animal runs out in front of him, and Charlie is decapitated by a telephone pole. Peter, in a state of shock, drives home and goes to bed. The next sound that occurs in the film is Annie's horrifying scream upon finding her daughter's body.

It is at this point in the movie that the audience comes to learn they are not just watching a typical horror movie and the reality of the film starts to become difficult to grasp. The locus of horror seems to lie with the mother, Annie, as she seeks out occult interventions in order to reconnect with Charlie. She slowly begins to unravel and there is a shift from a grieving mother to a possessed mother, as depicted in dream sequences/memories of her setting fire to herself and Peter, hiding in the corners of the room to spy on Charlie, and eventually cutting off her own head. There are several twists and turns the film takes to arrive at the conclusion, which has to do with a demonic possession and a cult. Though interesting in its own right, the story of the film is, in my opinion, richer when watched from the perspective of the son Peter, with a Lacanian lens. From this perspective, Peter seems to be suffering from a psychotic break, unable to escape the jouissance of the Other, manifesting in everything from his reflection smiling at him to being stalked by his mother throughout the house. What makes it more disturbing is that the audience is not necessarily able to tell the difference between Peter's perspective and Annie's, with shared dreams and miniature scenes blurring their subjectivities. Throughout the horror, stories are woven about Peter and his mother, specifically about how she did not want him and at one point sleepwalked into his room and tried to set him on fire. This omnipresent and threatening Other seems indicative of a psychotic structure, which Peter is able to knot in the end, by instantiating a delusional metaphor, namely, that his mother was in a cult and his body is now the house of the demon Paimon.

The reason that this movie functions so well as a social complaint is because of the inability of the father, Paul, to affect any sort of cut to Annie's jouissance. Even more telling, at one-point, Annie believes she is connected to Charlie's journal, and by burning the journal, she will burn herself alive, but save her family from being haunted. Instead, however, it is Paul who bursts into flames when the journal, and this should be understood as the Symbolic intervention, is burned. It is at this point that Annie's jouissance is unleased on Peter and he is no longer able to escape her and the members of her cult. With the different subplots, twists, and decoys, there is one constant from both the Peter's perspective and the audience's, Paul needs to stop Annie. The effect that this has on the audience is palpable. The theatre that I watched this film in felt airless, and many moviegoers who watched it remarked on forums that the film was relentless and that they felt they did not get the typical breaks from the tension that a traditional horror film allows. My partner, an avid horror movie lover, also remarked that he had to remind himself that this was "just a movie." The audience, like Peter, has no choice but to be slowly pulled into Annie's descent into madness, and also like Peter, the audience seems to be in the position of being looked at, while looking back, though sometimes through fingers. Actually, it is looking through our fingers that gets at the heart of the complaint—symbolic mediation. With Paul being an ineffective father, both the Peter and the audience are left scrambling to offer up something to Annie as a stand in for his/our being. Peter is only able to mediate her jouissance through a delusion, and the audience only gets its reprieve when it leaves the theatre and begins to process what it just encountered. Though it is fair to say the film left its own traces of Real in this particular moviegoer's subjectivity, as I needed to be escorted around my own house for a day or two less Toni Collette or my own mother be hiding in the shadows.

This is where I would like to turn briefly to another film that coincides well with the themes explored in *Hereditary* and will help to explicate how these films can be read as a symptom. Lars Von Trier's 2009 *Antichrist* starring Willem Dafoe as He and Charlotte Gainsbourg as She also depicts a woman's grief following the loss of her child. While He and She were making love, their son falls out of a window. He, a therapist, decides to take She to a cabin where they can do a combination of processing, exposure therapy, and lovemaking. He attempts to step firmly into the role of therapist to counsel his wife, and, similar to Paul, is devastatingly ineffective, mainly because he is routinely seduced by her, both sexually and subjectively, meaning his own reality starts to become blurred the more She seems to lose hold of her Symbolic. Interestingly, the motif of the natural world is intimately tied to the nature of Woman, with all the chaotic implications, with

She herself believing that all women are innately evil. It is revealed to He that the reason his son fell out of the window was because of a foot deformity, caused by She putting his shoes on the wrong feet for years, perhaps in an attempt to keep him from leaving her, and thus losing her Symbolic investment. When He confronts She, She accuses him of wanting to leave her, which she attempts to solve by bolting a grindstone to his foot. Later, during a flashback, it is revealed the She saw her son fall from the window, but did not act, thus confirming her innate evil. To compensate for this, She castrates herself, before He frees himself and strangles her.

The effects of these films seem to call notions of identity and even masculinity into question. A quick scan of forums dedicated to *Hereditary* in particular reveal some common trends—oppressive dread, nausea, and a loss of boundary between self and film, all reminiscent of Julia Kristeva's work on abjection, which she understands as a primary revulsion toward the mother's body prior to castration. In particular, there is a lot of confusion pertaining to the viewers own fear of the movie. Many remark that they watch tons of horror movies, are gorehounds, or purposely seek out films that are notably disturbing, and yet they were affected by *Hereditary* in particular, though I believe a case could be made for others as well, including *Antichrist*, as well as Darren Aronofsky's 2017 *Mother!* With these films, our sense of self, namely, what we believe we can tolerate or not, what scares us or not, our past experiences with such encounters becomes compromised and we are left bereft. Our claims on our selves, our small signifiers we offer up to the other in lieu of all we do not know is deemed unworthy. Horror then functions as an intermediary—it offers a complaint—"that was f-ed up," which we immediately attempt to recruit others with "you have to see it!"

To contrast these films against a movie that deals with similar content, Jennifer Kent's 2014 *The Babadook* also explores how grief unleashes the jouissance of the Other, leaving the young son attempting to navigate his mother and a dark presence in the house. The difference is that the mother enters into a covenant with this presence, the Babadook, which we can understand here as the encroaching law, where she keeps it in the basement and feeds it, allowing it to be the thing in her, outside of her. Though an excellent movie, the audience has a way to knot the entire experience together, and we leave the movie relatively unscathed. It may be worth noting that this film, unlike the films we have been focusing on, was written and directed by a woman, and in making a deal with the law demonstrates to some extent the feminine side of the sexual nonrelation. These other films, however, may signify a cultural complaint from the masculine side, when that pact is not made and the nonrelation is vulgarly exposed in the form of a paranoid truth that the woman in question belonged to some sort of cult of women, with their own secret knowledge to which no phallus will do. Such an anxiety is then realized when actual mothers do not act in accord with the supposed covenant they made with the law, which can be seen explicitly in the cases of mothers who murdered their children.

Murderous mothers

The morbid fascination with monstrous mothers has been known to transcend film and captivate the greater public via news stories and murder trials, with shows like *Nancy Grace* doggedly covering every tiny detail of both the trial and the lives of the family. Mothers who murder their children tend to receive greater attention by the national media, which implicit in this is the curiosity about why and how a mother in particular could do such a thing. In most of these cases, the woman's mental stability is called into question with diagnoses like postpartum stress and depression being thrown around by newscasters and lay people. However, as Hollandsworth (2001) points out, there is not the same sort of speculation when a man is the one to commit murder and there tends to be more of an emphasis on it as a violent act as opposed to a psychotic break on the part of the murderer. Skott-Myhre (2015) suggests why this may be the case, stating that there is an implicit assumption that women are nurturers and that to be "a happy woman" is dependent on how well she can sustain her role as a primary caregiver. She states further that instead of questioning the living conditions under which some women live, irritability and interpersonal conflicts are reduced to an assumption that the woman must be experiencing premenstrual disorder.

Such attempts to codify or explain why a woman is behaving the way she is speaks to the obsessional neurotic compulsion to explain away the unconscious of the Other. If she is experiencing some sort of chemical imbalance, then there is nothing I as the obsessional neurotic have for her. However, despite attempts to rationalize the cases of Susan Smith, Andrea Yates, or Casey Anthony, which I will explain in more detail shortly, the proliferation of discourses and fascination with these cases, even today, suggests that the knowledge used to account for this anxiety is not adequate. Hollandsworth (2001) points out that many people expressed sympathy for Yates, showing up to her house with flowers, and some women noting that they too have felt a depression that was scarily close to what Yates had described. This phenomenon echoes what Freidan (1963) had been saying many years earlier about "the problem which has no name," referring to the overwhelming and widespread depression that stay-at-home mothers or housewives were experiencing. It became fairly common to see women as being depressed or needing to cope with this type of depression, with pharmaceutical pills such as Prozac, Valium, and Xanax being casually referred to as "mommy's little blue pill" (Blum and Stracuzzi, 2004). However, in turning to a biomedical understanding of her suffering, it is assumed that the job of the wife and mother should be satisfying in and of itself and an experience of depression while one was living out one's duties as a woman was (and is still to some degree) indicative of psychopathology. In looking at the specific cases previously mentioned, it can also be argued that there is latent anxiety in the socius present, which may hint at some of Freud's, and to some extent Lacan's, to account for woman once again.

The cases

In the fall of 1994, Susan Smith reported to South Carolina police that her car had been stolen with her two children, three-year-old Michael and fourteen-month-old, Alexander, inside. She told the police that an African American man had driven away with her children inside, and for the nine days that followed, she pleaded on the media for their return. However, it was discovered that she had strapped her children into the back seat of her car and rolled it into a lake, drowning her children. She claimed to not have a motive, though speculations were made that she did it for a boyfriend who had recently broke up with her, and that she was not in her right mind. Though a psychiatrist diagnosed her with dependent personality disorder and major depressive disorder, her defense lawyer agreed that she did in fact know right from wrong and she was deemed legally sane. Though there were demands for the death penalty, Smith was sentenced to life in prison (Ford, 1996).

A few years later, in 2001, in Houston, Texas, Andrea Yates called the police to come to her home. When they arrived, she led them to her bedroom in which four of her five children were laid out on the bed, while the fifth child was still in the bathtub. She explained calmly to the police that she had drowned them one by one in her bathtub. When the police asked her why she had done it, she remarked that she felt that they were not developing normally, and so she decided to send them to God (Hollandsworth, 2001). She was tried twice after the prosecution's psychiatrist and witness admitted he had given false information. Dr. Park Dietz was also a consultant on the show *Law and Order*, and he remarked that because Yates was an avid watcher of the show, she likely would have seen the episode in which a mother drowned her children and then pled insanity, giving her the idea. This would merit a rejection of an insanity plea for Yates, as by watching the show, she would have had an indication of right from wrong, and thus not legally insane. Dr. Dietz, however, was wrong as this episode did not air until three years after the murders and when the case was appealed, it was agreed that the jury could have been persuaded by this. Yates' verdict was then changed from guilty and 40 years in prison, to not guilty by reason of insanity, and she was moved to a mental health treatment facility (O'Malley, 2005). Disturbing in its own right, this demonstrates the more explicit ways in which the media is intimately interwoven in our own projections.

In both the cases of Andrea Yates and Susan Smith, both women admitted to killing their children, and both were spared the death penalty, though there had been precedent for it. Furthermore, both of these cases produced a series of narratives about both women. Their struggles, their heartbreak, the abuse they faced as children, the cruelty of their partners, was all detailed in varying descriptions in newspaper and television programs. Looking back on this data and footage, there seems to be an overwhelming desire to analyze these women's lives for the purposes of attempting to understand why they murdered their children. Meyers and Oberman (2001) explain that these narratives tend to emphasize the woman as either "mad" or "bad," with the mad mothers portrayed as ultimately good mothers, but their crimes as irrational or out of character, whereas the bad women were portrayed as cold and callous, neglected their children, and had their perceived immoral behavior emphasized. In the case of Susan Smith, members of the jury remarked that they had felt that she was a very disturbed person and the death penalty would not have been just (Meyers and Oberman, 2001). Psychoanalyst Melanie Klein remarks about this split of the good and bad mother. Klein (1987) argues that the infant splits the mother into the good and bad object, or more specifically, the good and bad breast. The good breast is the breast that is available and nurturing, whereas the bad breast is the one the infant experiences the mother as persecutory or hostile. The splitting between the mother and the woman, however, is first identified by Freud (1957) in what he referred to as the Madonna-Whore complex, in which the woman is split between their love object, the Madonna, and the object of their desire, the Whore. While this theory has been written about at length, it seems to be relevant in those cases in which the mother and the woman are at odds with one another. Feminist theorists have argued that such a dichotomy exists within women themselves, as they have internalized the male gaze. I would like to suggest that this confusion about what a woman wants, or is, is exacerbated in the attempts to lay out a narrative about these women, and that as soon as the question of the Woman's desire within the mother is encroached upon, the narrative seemingly becomes too disturbing for falls apart.

It is important to note that "not being in her right mind" or being disturbed is not a clinical diagnosis and therefore not grounds for an insanity plea, and yet it is what allowed the jurors to feel sympathy for Smith. Kristeva (1982) refers to narratives as "an elaborate attempt, next to syntactic competence, to situate a speaking being between his desires and their prohibitions" (p. 140). In constructing a narrative around these women, one in which they take part in, the symbolic representation of Woman comes to include a distinct form of suffering and pathology. This version of the feminine monster reaffirms the castrated woman, and the horror of her actions is intimately entangled with the pathos of her character. In both of these cases, references to the neglectful or absent fathers are emphasized, with the assumption that had they done their job by merely being present, with emphasis here on the phallic presence, or law, that would have been able to mediate in some way. The further assumption here then is that the absence of this phallus, paternal metaphor, or Law is what causes these women to act in such a way. The narratives, as Kristeva said, serve as a way to locate the speaking being, by reinstating the missing phallus. This is done in several ways, usually appealing to psychological discourse and the public's familiarity with what constitutes psychological trauma. References were made to both Yates' and Smith's childhood traumas, complete with sexual abuse and neglect, that Smith had witnessed a suicide and Yates was a victim of harsh religious ideologies. Finally for both women, postpartum depression and postpartum psychosis became a popular explanation; one which pathologized, rather than demonized the mothers, allowing for a belief that they would have been better mothers had they had the appropriate medical intervention.

However, as Soler (2003) explains, when considering the desire of the woman in the figure of the mother, "the not-whole remains, by definition, silent; it is an absolute silence that haunts everything that is ordered in the phallic series" (p. 121). If the mother who loves her child too much to the point of psychosis is at one end of the pole, then the mother who cares nothing for her child to the point of neglect is at the other, which becomes its own particular construction of monstrosity. It is not fair to say that Smith or Yates were neglectful or did not care for their children, as up until the point they murdered them, family and friends remarked on how well the children were loved and cared for (Hollandsworth, 2001). However, the disturbing nature of their crimes seem to demand explanations that index their inabilities to be good mothers. Yates told police that she was sending her children to God—an act of love. Yates, on the other hand, seemingly strays too far from the desire of the mother and the desire for something beyond the child, to the point of (perhaps momentarily, as she claimed she was not in her right mind) having nothing to do with them at all. In fact, what is demonstrated in both cases, and perhaps what evokes the simultaneous sympathy and horror, is the ambivalence these women, as opposed to mothers, had toward their children. Attempts to explain this through postpartum depression or major depressive disorder then mask this ambivalence for the phallus, which was supposed to satisfy the desire of the woman, at the heart of these cases.

It is this ambivalence that evokes horror because the Other's desire cannot be satisfied through conventional neurotic compromises, that is, the phallus as a stand in for the person's being. When confronted with the question "What does the Other want from me?" and the answer following Freud was "a phallus of her own," then these women suggest that this too may not be enough. Soler explains that the mother of the unconscious, that is the mother unconsciously experienced, as opposed to the actual mother, risks being a too-mothering mother or a too-womanly mother, occupied elsewhere and unrecognizable to the child/spectator. In being too-womanly, Soler means that a part of her desire lies outside of the Symbolic, as in the cases of the mystics according to Lacan. While the mystics were said to experience beyond the Symbolic, in this case being in the form of God's intermediaries, such as the Pope or members of the clergy, the dissatisfaction with the phallus in these cases lies in what their children are unable to do for them, namely subjectivize them as mothers. As mentioned, this is the issue of the woman's desire within the mother that Lacan attempts to reconcile with Freud's question and thus, it is in cases like this that one of the most recurring and established means of subjectivizing Woman and her desire, that is, Woman as mother, also fails to account for the Other.

Obsessive neurotics and their mothers

In returning briefly to the idea of an obsessional neurotic, I would like to argue that it is possible to psychoanalyze Psychoanalysis's representation of mothers through a Lacanian framework. Though analysts may take a particular role in the actual psychoanalytic session, the proliferation of texts and the production of knowledge regarding phalluses, jouissance, and the role of the primary caregivers seems to demonstrate what Lacan would refer to as an obsessional project. This is especially true when it is taken into consideration the time and energy that is spent among analysts debating which term or theory better speaks to the experience of the analysand as demonstrated in the publication of several journals and books, not to mention conferences, summits, and lectures. With psychoanalysis as an obsessional project, the theorizations regarding the m(O)ther attempts to answer the question "What does the Other want from me?" with knowledge about the Other. Though the analyst as theorist does not take the place of the obsessional in the sense that he denies the unconscious, he does take the position of assuming that he can produce a knowledge about the unconscious and that he can give an account of his own. As Fink (1999) explains, the obsessive believes himself to be a whole subject without a lack and refusing to acknowledge his dependence on the Other.

In regard to sexual partners, each is interchangeable for the next and the partner becomes transformed into a maternal figure (Fink, 1999). This is also what psychoanalysis falls susceptible to as well. The maternal figure is a function in psychoanalytic theory, and the human subject within that function becomes interchangeable. Fink goes on to explain that Freud identified a tendency in what would become the obsessional neurotic subject to classify women as either the Madonna or the whore, "the mother figure who can be loved and adored versus the exciting woman who embodies object a, who cannot be transformed into a maternal object" (p. 123). Psychoanalysis seems to have an equally ambivalent relationship to mothers, emphasizing the disastrous consequences of being too close to her, while also further establishing her responsibility in relation to the development of the infant. Jacqueline Rose's (2018) recent book highlights this facet of psychoanalysis, while also expounding on the inescapable and intimate relationship to mother that we both individually and collectively share. She argues that the mother becomes the localization of our idealization and grievances, entrenching us in a relationship of cruelty. Psychoanalysis perhaps best elucidates this in theory with the mother of the unconscious at the same time the site of love and affection, as well as the object which will never return and sets us up for constant disappointment. The result is that there is an abundance of discourses on the role of the mother in the subject's unconscious that serves to buffer against the actual desire and unconscious of the woman as mother. Psychoanalysis localizes the question of sexual difference as being in relation the jouissance of the mother, thus positing the threat of sexual difference as stemming from her, and further organizing the desire of the woman as implicitly the desire of the mother. I would like to note here, however, that though the theory may reflect this, the practice of analysis would undoubtedly challenge some of these preconceptions, if they so should arise, hence marking another difficulty in separating theory from the praxis.

Deterritorializing the woman-mother

In Seminar XX, Lacan himself explained that psychoanalysis has not been able to account for the desire of the Woman, suggesting that the idea of Woman is always contextualized and in relation to phallic pronouncements. As explained earlier, Deleuze and Guattari (1980) refers to this adherence to a particular manifestation of subjectivity as a molarized identity and limits the amount of desire that can circulate in the subject. "Mother" has become a prominent method of subjectivizing women, though I will argue later it cannot be completely captured in discourse, which inevitably leads to a productive surplus. Mothering and the mother as identity has been researched, legislated, and discussed in several ways. Parenting classes, breastfeeding tutorials, research on epigenetics, maternity clothes, not to mention psychological research including the effects of helicopter parenting, attachment styles, language acquisition and development, etc. discursively outline the contours of what a mother is and should be. Though attempts to present a more gender-neutral approach to issues of parenting have become more prominent, research has emphasized how what can be done for women to balance work with parenting demands, or how certain careers affect their abilities to parent (Hibel, Mercado and Trumbell, 2012; Cooklin, Westrupp, Strazdins, Giallo, Martin and Nicholson, 2015; Lee, McHale, Crouter, Hammer and Almeida, 2017). Such attempts to define "mother" position her in opposition to the role of "father," and as object of the infant, as posited by psychoanalysis, emphasizing binaries premised in identities that need to be cultivated and established in relation to a series of I/Other cuts. The notion of mother then comes to function symbolically as a particular type of woman, specifically the type of woman that Freud eluded to: a woman who has finally reclaimed her phallus. This conceptualization then ignores the generative power and potential in the actual woman-infant assemblage. In considering the case of Andrea Yates in particular, but also her sympathizers, as well as Susan Smith, the violent nature of shedding a seemingly concretized subjectification is demonstrated.

It is not my intention here to romanticize the suffering that caused and were caused by these tragic cases, nor is it now my intention to advocate that women should behave similarly in order to shed their role as mother. Furthermore, I am not suggesting that there is something wrong with being a mother, that having a child is somehow anti-feminist, or that women cannot experience a great deal of joy from being a mother. Rather, it has been my intention to demonstrate the ways in which assumptions about the

Woman's desire within the mother role have produced monstrous women as a symptom. That is, by assigning a particular signifier to the cause of the Woman's desire, the ways in which this signifier will also fail are also implicit in this designation. While some of the attempts to account for this failure have been to think through the effects the mother will have on the child as phallus, whether it be in creating a psychotically or perversely structured subject, these attempts have still failed to consider the ways in which Woman's desire will continue to evade subjective capture. It is this evasion that I turn to now as a means to think through the potential women like Andrea Yates and Susan Smith had in shifting the unconscious assumptions and discourses about sexual difference and what constitutes a Woman's desire.

To begin, it is important to emphasize, as Braidotti (2011) does, that the term "mother" can be opened up to not only include women who have birthed or adopted children, but also to include a consideration of the maternal function of women, which then applies to a discursive field women inhabit, regardless of whether or not they have children. This discursive field posits woman as mother essentially, which actual women must respond to in several ways, whether it be by taking "mother" on as an identity or by failing to respond adequately or not at all. Even in responding by saying "I choose not to be a mother" the woman still responds to the discursive field of the maternal function and thus reinforces its organizing and subjectivizing power. In order to conceive of a politics that challenges subjectivization, it then must not respond to this maternal function, and if the maternal function according to Freud is to endow the woman with a phallus of her own, then it also must not rely on an affirmation of presence.

In the cases of Andrea Yates and Susan Smith, not to mention several other women in similar situations, attempts to diagnose these women with mental disorders is an attempt to bestow on them a new phallus, one truer than the other had been. The rationale being that they were unable to attend to, care for, appreciate appropriately their phalluses as children because they already had phalluses as postpartum depression or major depressive disorder. Their subjectivity had already been constituted. I would like to suggest that this type of codification, that of psychiatric diagnoses, of the feminine subject becomes a popular and even sought after means of indoctrinating women more fully into phallic logic. I will argue this more substantially in the chapter on borderline personality disorder, but disorders dominated by feminine subjects, and I do want to be explicit about feminine subjects versus females here, tend to revolve around this question of feminine desire and the failure to adequately symbolize that which is lacking. These disorders, such as bipolar disorder, dependent personality disorder, postpartum depression, borderline personality disorder, and major depressive disorder seem to rely on a failure of an object or person as object to satisfy the individual's desire, and thus rely on an essential excessiveness.

However, latent in this is the fact that both Yates and Smith demonstrated that there was something more to the desire of woman than a phallus of her own, at least a phallus in the form of a child. More troubling, not only did these women not want their children, but also they took the steps necessary to destroy them. Mothers have left their children and families before, and it tends to be met with more outrage than when the father does it, but Yates and Smith went a step further, and yet, were met with sympathy. Rather than disowning their children and addressing their maternal function, these women took a step toward deterritorializing their subjectivity so that they were no longer in relation to their maternal function.

M(O)ther as nexus.

In their combined projects, *Anti-Oedipus* (1972) and *A Thousand Plateaus* (1980), Deleuze and Guattari utilize the schizophrenic, as Lacan's psychotic, to rethink the unconscious outside of the psychoanalytic neurotic project. The schizophrenic subject allows them to think of schizophrenia as a form of thought, and the subject as a revolutionary figure, "liberating life and desire from their capture in ideological and repressive systems, the machinery of social reproduction, with all the risk this entails" (Schuster, 2016, p. 32). The psychotic subject is the subject prior to a neurotic structure, which Deleuze and Guattari identify as a particular manifestation of subjectivity in which the abundant flow of desire has been caught in a repetitive Oedipal drama. In fact, they argue that the family drama as posited by psychoanalysis is a form of colonization, relegating subjects with potential for all types of assemblages to identities which allow little room for experimentation or creativity. The nuclear family, they argue, is a capitalist institution, which is delegated the function of reproduction, and not simply the reproduction of the species, but of subjects which adhere to capitalist demands (Holland, 2005). In contrast, the psychotically structured person demonstrates a method of thought that engages with pre-Oedipal subjectivity specifically because it relies on the foreclosure of the aforementioned paternal metaphor that pulls the subject from the assemblage of part objects, castrating him and creating a circuit of desire.

In this reconceptualization of schizophrenia, the mother also occupies a similar spot as in the Lacanian formulations of structuration, but the potential for creative experimentation is different. The mother is instead the first assemblage of desiring-machines that the infant is able to encounter. She is the site of generativity, which as explained by Lacan, can also be too much for the infant at times, but this allows him or her to disconnect and reconnect, forming new ways to come back and leave, experimenting with how his or her partial objects connect with others and evaluating the contingencies that stimulate of inhibit desire. Massumi (1992) suggests that the psychoanalytic assumption that this pre-Oedipal subjectivity encounter with the m(O)ther is a time of desperate confusion and a sense of fragmentation are projected onto the body of the infant, further cutting his or her experiences into dialectics. He states,

> What lies outside Oedipal subjectivity (actually, beside it: it is always contemporaneous with identity even if it is submerged by it) is an effective superposition of an unaccustomed range of pragmatic potentials, not a protometaphysical 'confusion.' A return to the body without organs is actually a return of fractality, a resurfacing of the virtual.
>
> (p. 85)

A return to this fractality is also a return to a particular relationship to the m(O)ther, which challenges an assumption that the encounter with the m(O)ther is the cause of pathology, and instead asks how this encounter may actually possess potential for surplus desire and generativity. This is not to say, of course, that neurotics do not actually exist, and that the discoveries made by Lacan and his descendants on the analyst's couch are inaccurate. Nor am I attempting to suggest that mothers have no role in the mental suffering of their children. Patriarchal standards for women still place the responsibility of raising children largely on them, and it is inevitable that they will struggle in ways that will have a direct effect on their children's lives. The question, however, is how to divert this recapitulation of the same Oedipal drama, the same neurotic habits which ground women as m(O)ther, and their children as perpetually attempting to possess and escape the mother.

Bracha Ettinger, Lacanian psychoanalyst and artist, offers a means through which to think through about the neurotic unconscious as co-arising with element of the unconscious that resembles Deleuze and Guattari's Body with Organs. Ettinger (2006) conceives of the matrixial borderspace, which refers to a supplementary part of the unconscious that is not constituted by the phallus, but rather the uterus as a means to discuss relationality between subjects. The borderspace refers to the shared body of the mother/fetus in which both subjects are in relation to the other, and simultaneously composed of an "I" and a "not I." These, like other experiences according to psychoanalytic theory, are repressed, only to return through speech acts or behaviors. The return of the matrixial is through instantaneous and fleeting encounters with the Other, in which there is no clear distinction between subjects. For Ettinger, this matrixial experience is also represented in the Symbolic, but not in language and its castrating nature, but rather through images, art, and embodied resonances, which would typically be relegated to the psychotic in the traditional psychotic paradigm. Ettinger cautions against this and instead understands such experiences and ways of knowing as an initiation in jointness and can be seen in traditional feminine ways of knowing, such as intuition, shared trauma, telepathy, and inspiration. It is in these practices and ways of knowing in which the subject as constituted by the womb can be understood as the simultaneous I/not-I, that is affected and affecting the other in a co-constitution of subjectivity, something that predates any sort of Lacanian cut.

Ettinger argues that this brand of subjectivity is not only marginalized but, in some cases, also pathologized, because it challenges our conceptualizations of the bounded and autonomous individual that is self-determined because of this linking with the unknown and bounding with unknown others in the process of becoming and transforming oneself. Ettinger thus rethinks the unconscious, which allows for a consideration of this schizophrenia Deleuze and Guattari advocate, which effects a trace in all individuals, not just feminine subjects, and as Skott-Myhre (2017) points out, rethinks subjectivity as primarily developing between a mother and child affiliation in utero, with the injunction of Symbolic demands as secondary. Recent research in neurobiology also suggests that the separation of mother and child is never quite as distinct as we tend to believe, with not only the child possessing the DNA of the mother, but also the mother containing cells of the child in her brain (Martone, 2012). Not only does Ettinger's theory suggest a way to consider the encounter between child and mother as more than the production of neurosis or psychosis, though it may occur alongside it, but she also provides a way to consider sexual difference outside of the phallic signifier. As Cavanagh (2016) remarks in her piece on transsexuality as sinthome, Ettinger's borderlinking is an event in the Real, making the Other jouissance responsive to an unsymbolized encounter between mother and fetus, which produces affects and inscriptions in the matrixial substratum. From this perspective, sexual difference constituted by a borderspace and a linking of borders offers a unique perspective to rethink subjectivity outside of phallic arrangement. I will argue in the next chapter, however, that this borderlinking also produces encounters that are anxiety provoking, specifically because of Ettinger's claim that this feminine borderspace is repressed in all individuals, which means when it surfaces, it has the potential to reorganize subjectivity in a way that is unfamiliar. It is specifically this anxiety and unfamiliarity that I will take up in considering sexual difference in the era of the capitalist superegoic demand to enjoy through the subject within the diagnosis of borderline personality disorder in the final chapter.

References

Aronson, A. (2019, May). Accelerationism and ordinary psychosis: The psychical contingencies of post-capitalist utopia. Paper presented at Lack iii. Psychoanalysis and Separation conference in Worcester, Massachusetts.

Blum, L.M. and Stracuzzi, N.F. (2004). Gender in the prozac nation: Popular discourse and productive femininity. *Gender and Society, 18*(3), 269–286.

Braidotti, R. (2011). *Nomadic subjects: Embodiment and sexual difference in contemporary feminist theory.* New York: Columbia University Press.

Cavanagh, S.L. (2016). Transsexuality as sinthome: Bracha L. Ettinger and the other (feminine) sexual difference. *Studies in Gender and Sexuality, 17*(1), 27–44.

Ceitan, K., Moliere, K., Producers. and Kent, J. (2014). *The Babadook.* Sydney, Australia: Entertainment One.

Cooklin, A.R., Westrupp, E., Strazdins, L., Giallo, R., Martin, A. and Nicholson, J.M. (2015). Mothers' work-family conflict and enrichment: Associations with parenting quality and couple relationship. *Child: Care, Health and Development, 41*(2), 266–277.

Deleuze, G. and Guattari, F. (1972). *Anti-Oedipus: Capitalism and schizophrenia.* London: Penguin Classics.

Deleuze, G. and Guattari, F. (1980). *A thousand plateaus: Capitalism and schizophrenia.* Minneapolis: University of Minnesota Press.

Ettinger, B. (2006). *The matrixial borderspace.* Minneapolis: University of Minnesota Press.

Felman, S. (1993). *What does a woman want? Reading and sexual difference.* Baltimore: The John Hopkins University Press.

Fink, B. (1996). *The Lacanian subject: Between language and jouissance.* Princeton: Princeton University Press.

Fink, B. (1999). *A clinical introduction to Lacanian psychoanalysis: Theory and technique.* New York: Routledge.

Foldager, M.L., Producer. and Von Trier, L., Director. (2009). *Antichrist.* Denmark: Nordisk Film Distribution.

Ford, J. (1996). Susan Smith and other homicidal mothers: In search of the punishment that fits the crime. *Cardozo Women's Law Journal, 3*(1), 521–548.

Freidan, B. (1973). *The feminine mystique.* New York: W.W. Norton & Co.

Freud, S. (1957). A special type of choice of object made by men. In J. Strachey's (Ed.), *The standard edition of the complete works of Sigmund Freud, volume XI (1910)* (163–176). London: The Hogarth Press and the Institute of Psychoanalysis.

Freud, S. (2010). Femininity. In L.G. Fiorini and G.A. Sas Rose (Eds.), *On Freud's femininity* (7–34). New York: Routledge. (Original work published in 1933).

Gherovici, P. (2014). Where have the hysterics gone? Lacan's reinvention of hysteria. *English Studies in Canada, 40*(1), 47–70.

Hibel, L.C., Mercado, E. and Trumbell, J.M. (2012). Parenting stressors and cortisol levels in a sample of working mothers. *Journal of Family Psychology, 26*(5), 738–746.

Holland, E.W. (2005). *Deleuze and Guattari's Anti-Oedipus: Introduction to schizoanalysis.* New York: Routledge.

Hollandsworth, S. (2001, August). Her dark places. *Texas Monthly, 29*(8), 114–118.

Klein, M. (1987). A contribution to the psychogenesis of manic-depressive states. In J. Mitchell's (Ed.), *The selected Melanie Klein* (115–145). New York: Free Press. (Original work published in 1935).

Knudsen, L., Frakes, K.S., Patrick, B., Producers. and Aster, A., Director. (2018). *Hereditary.* Los Angeles: A24 Films.

Kristeva, J. (1982). *Powers of horror: An essay on abjection.* New York: Columbia University Press.

Lacan, J. (1998). *The four fundamental concepts of psychoanalysis: Book XI.* New York: W.W. Norton & Co.

Lacan, J. (2015). *On the names of the father.* Cambridge: Polity.

Lacan, J. (2016). *Anxiety: Book X.* Cambridge: Polity.

Lacan, J. (2019). *Desire and its interpretation: The seminar of Jacques Lacan: Book VI*. Cambridge: Polity.

Lee, S., McHale, S.M., Crouter, A.C., Hammer, L.B. and Almeida, D.M. (2017). Finding time over time: Longitudinal links between employed mothers' work-family conflict and time profiles. *Journal of Family Psychology, 31*(5), 604–615.

Martone, R.L. (2012, December 4). Scientists discover children's cells living in mothers' brains. *Scientific American*. Retrieved from https://www.scientificamerican.com/article/scientists-discover-childrens-cells-living-in-mothers-brain/ (Accessed March 8 2020 and June 10 2019).

Massumi, B. (1992). *A user's guide to capitalism and schizophrenia: Deviations from Deleuze and Guattari*. Cambridge: The MIT Press.

Meyers, C.L. and Oberman, M. (2001). *Mothers who kill their children: Understanding the acts of moms from Susan Smith to the "Prom Mom"*. New York: New York University Press.

Rose, J. (2018). *Mothers: An essay on love and cruelty*. New York: Farrar, Straus and Giroux.

Schuster, A. (2016). *The trouble with pleasure: Deleuze and psychoanalysis*. Cambridge: The MIT Press.

Skott-Myhre, K. (2015). The feminization of labor and the DSM-5. *Annual Review of Critical Psychology, 12*, 71–78.

Skott-Myhre, K. (2017). *Feminist spirituality under capitalism: Witches, fairies and nomads*. London: Routledge.

Soler, C. (2003). *What Lacan said about women: A psychoanalytic study*. New York: Other Press.

Chapter 6

Fairytales and femme fatales

In contrast to the mother-monster, in which there is a conflation of the woman's desire with the mother's, the characterization of femme fatales represents a character that is exceptionally the figure of Woman. If the mother is redeemed by obtaining her own phallus through which to mediate her excess jouissance, the femme fatale is the woman who shirks any conciliation with such an intervention and instead plunges into her inevitable destruction, taking victims as she goes. She is the locus of sexuality and death, and becomes a common trope in film noir during the 1940s and 1950s. Sobchak (1998) suggests that this genre of film became popular in the 1940s because it reflected the pessimistic post-World War II era, while Johnson (2009) argues that the femme fatale specifically reflects men's fears about women who were liberated during the war. The femme fatale seems to have served as a sublimation of anxieties about sexuality and death, while also providing a figure for many women to identify with or admire. I would like to suggest that the femme fatale becomes a figure through which young girls and women both identify, and are encouraged to reject, as well as serve as a cultural touchstone about the danger of the male desire in relation to the Woman. In doing so, it is my contention that the femme fatale, as represented in both the film noir tradition, and also in children's fairytales, embody the complicated relationship between sex and death that feminine subjects are more closely in confrontation with and provide a means through which to think about the melancholia that constitutes the feminine position as posited by Kristeva (1992). The role of the audience then becomes an important factor in considering the question about sexual difference manifested in this particular characterization of Woman.

The melancholic feminine

In order to understand the significance the femme fatale can have on the subjective development of young girls and women, especially as it pertains to the differences between the sexes, I return to Kristeva and her understanding of the suppression of the feminine. In formulating her notion of the abject, Kristeva argues that there is an unconscious move away from the mother that is reinforced in the symbolic killing of the mother, or cultural matricide. Following Freud, she believes that the loss of the maternal object is disturbing, though necessary for the development of the ego (Kristeva, 1982). The subject then mourns the lost object through creative linguistic expression, or what Lacan refers to as phallic jouissance, with the idea of mourning demonstrating both the loss of the object, and the loss of desire in the face of the object. Kristeva suggests that it is a loving father who facilitates this transition from mother to language, which I would like to qualify by suggesting that what is necessary to ease this transition is a symbolic intervention that seems to hint at the desire of the mother. In contrast, melancholia, Kristeva notes, is the inability to let go of the lost object and instead, a self is built around the dead mother. The mother, of course, may still be alive, but in this sense, dead, rather than repressed, conveys a specific relationship. The dead mother, in contrast with the lost maternal object which necessitates creative expression, is a loss of vitality and generativity when the mother's desire is unable to be symbolized and to which the subject in question always refers.

For Kristeva, young girls are particularly prone to formulating a self constituted by melancholia. This is due to the tenuous relationship feminine subjects have with language and the difficulty they have in identifying with a signifier. Soler (2003) further explicates this trouble with development in her elaboration on the feminine side of the Oedipus complex, in which the young girl, being unable to misrecognize her possession of the phallus, must then also identify with her mother, whose subjectivity is also organized around a lack, thus lack must identify with lack. Inherent to the feminine position is an apprehension of death, though not formulated in a question about the death of the self as demonstrated in obsessional neurosis, but rather a subject who preens loss. Such a character is presented to young children, girls in particular, in fairytales and stories at the exact time that they are to reconcile with this discovery. In particular, the evil queen or evil stepmother in fairytales is offered to young girls as an aid in their moral development. I would like to suggest that the evil queen of fairytales, and their contemporary reiterations, serve as feminine monster specifically curated with qualities that index this particular developmental period in feminine subjects as a way to usher them through to a subjectivity predicated on phallic investment. According to Freud, this means via a male baby for the woman, but from a Lacanian perspective, this could also mean that the woman stakes a claim in Symbolic meaning and law. The character in these tales that fails to do so, most notably the evil queen or stepmother, serves as an early example of the femme fatale, which is then reiterated in several narratives.

Characterization of the femme fatale

The femme fatale can be identified by several characteristics, regardless of the genre or medium she appears in. She is usually a young to middle age adult woman, who is either single or is married to a man whom she overpowers and is rendered useless both to her and the narrative. The femme fatale character is always remarkably beautiful, so much so that the men in her presence tend to compulsively remark about her appearance and the effect it has on them. She tends to be unaware of her beauty and her influence over men, though it is usually revealed later that she knows full well the effect that she has over men. She entices others with her sexuality to fulfill her demands, which are usually a means to her own and all involved, destruction.

With these traits considered, it is easy to see how there are several female figures represented in popular culture that fit the femme fatale motif but do not belong to film noir. Jancovich (2008) has argued earlier that the femme fatale figure has been used to describe a figure exclusively in film noir, but actually transcends several genres, though with more or less of the defining characteristics represented in the film noir tradition. Several horror films, such as *Misery, Friday the 13th,* and *Urban Legend* feature female murderers, who not only kill but do so through sophisticated manipulation and usually to satisfy a desire they can no longer be accountable for. Another genre that is particularly relevant to the current discussion is children's fairytales, in which the femme fatale is characterized as the evil queen, or stepmother in some cases. Though there are several fairytales that feature a diabolical woman or women torturing children, virgins, and men, I will limit my discussion to the most well-known, thanks to Disney and contemporary nostalgia for children's stories retold for adults: the Evil Queen in *Snow White*.

The Evil Queen and Snow White

The Evil Queen is a character in the Brothers Grimm story "Snow White." Snow White's mother dies giving birth to her and her father, the King, remarries a jealous and vain woman who possesses a magic mirror. Every morning the new queen asks the mirror who is the fairest of them all, and the mirror confirms that it is her, until Snow White, now older, replaces her as the fairest. The queen becomes enraged and orders a huntsman to kill Snow White, and bring back her lungs and liver as proof she is dead. The huntsman becomes captivated by Snow and is unable to complete the task and instead brings the queen the organs of a boar, while Snow escapes to the woods, eventually finding a cabin of dwarves to live with. Believing Snow to be the dead, the queen once again asks the mirror who is the fairest of them all, and it once more replies "Snow White," alerting the queen that Snow is still alive. The queen then takes on several disguises, such as an old peddler and a comb seller, to poison Snow White, but she is always saved just in time by the dwarves. Finally, the queen dresses up as an old woman and gives Snow a poisoned apple. The dwarves are unable to revive her this time, and believing she is dead, place her in a glass case. She remains perfectly preserved, as she is not dead, but in a coma. Sometime later, a prince is passing by and asks for Snow's coffin so that he can carry her to a proper resting place. As the dwarves are transporting her, one of them trips and jostles the coffin, causing the apple to be dislodged from her throat. The prince, immediately charmed by her, proposes and he and Snow are married. The queen, unable to abstain from her jealousy, attends the wedding where she is presented with iron shoes just removed from burning coals. The prince forces her to dance in the shoes until she dies.

This fairy tale represents a struggle, usually between a literal dead mother and a stepmother who is bent on her own and the child's destruction. The stepmother or Evil Queen is depicted as being tormented by her own lack, and thus provides an early femme fatale reference for the reader, usually assumed to be a female child. Snow, positioned between two mothers, and thus her own grief and lack, and a mission to kill the Evil Queen and replace her with herself. A traditional interpretation of the fairy tale suggests that it is a cautionary tale about giving in to envy and vanity. However, the relationship between Snow and the Evil Queen, and the omnipresent dead mother, allows for an interpretation that considers the mother–daughter relationship and the transmission of what it means to be a Woman. The Evil Queen is constituted by what she does not have, and ruminates on this, and can therefore be considered an example of Kristeva's melancholic subject. Her envy is predicated on something she did not receive from her own mother—that is, whatever would make her the fairest. The dead mother is the mother who is unable to offer the child a way through melancholia by placing her desire elsewhere, which subsequently leads to an interpretation that desire and death of desire are mutually exclusive. This is what makes the Evil Queen not only a femme fatale, but a femme fatale directed at young girls about the danger of feminine desire.

There have been several attempts to recreate and reimagine the Snow White story for film and television, each of which wrestle with feminine lack in unique ways. I will focus on three in particular due to their popularity and similar themes: Disney's *Snow White and the Seven Dwarfs* (1937), *Snow White and the Huntsman* (2012), and the depiction of the evil queen as Regina in ABC's television series *Once Upon a Time* (2011–2018). In each of these adaptations, the Evil Queen is juxtaposed against the fair Snow White, as per the original story. However, each of these new reiterations portrays the Evil Queen as in possession of magic, something not included in the original Brothers Grimm tale. For example, in the Disney version, the apple is not poisoned, but enchanted, implying that magic, not science is the culprit. In *The Huntsman*, Charlize Theron as the Evil Queen requires Snow's organs to remain young forever, suggesting she is involved in some dark arts. Finally, in the ABC version, the Evil Queen has a gift for magic that develops through lessons with Rumpelstiltskin, which she uses to put Snow White under a sleeping curse.

The addition of magic and, her ability to wield it, adds even more nuance to the Evil Queen as femme fatale, as well as points to the latent content pertaining to anxiety about sexual difference in the fairytale as fantasy. As mentioned, the Evil Queen functions as one of Snow White's mothers and thus demonstrating Freud's Madonna-Whore complex, in which he suggests that there are always two mothers of the unconscious. The stepmother, in this case, is the bad mother who not only instrumentalizes the father, but also casts him aside so she can go beyond him, meaning she exercises power beyond the parameters of her title as decreed upon her by marriage. With this in mind, magic can be understood as jouissance beyond the phallus. This is not to say that the Evil Queen is experiencing feminine jouissance, but like I suggested in the previous chapters, the ways she is represented seems to suggest that her desire lies elsewhere, and no substitution will do, suggesting a fantasy about such women. This becomes further illustrated in the numerous scenes in *Once* and *The Huntsman* in particular, in which she is offered something else in exchange for her revenge, whether it be the love of a man willing to tolerate her evil ways, or a truce with Snow, and though tempted, she is always possessed by a desire for something not satisfied in a reconciliation. Reconciliation can be also be understood here as submitting to the law, though the possession of magic would mean she is only partially subsumed by the law, making her partially castrated. Typically, revenge would be an example of phallic jouissance. However, for the Evil Queen, revenge always relies on her magic and is therefore, too much and something almost impossible to defend against as it cannot be localized. In *Once*, for example, the most damaging forms of magic, magic that threatens to take the townspeople's identities by erasing their memories and moving them to a new land, is in the form of colored clouds that infiltrate the town like a gas. Several scenes depict the Queen regretting her decision to use magic, but she is powerless against its reach once it is unleashed. Magic, like the jouissance of the femme fatale of the film noir, is what leads to the Evil Queen's own destruction.

In contrast, Snow's reputation as virtuous and dutiful is in direct contrast to the Evil Queen. In *Once*, Snow White even sneaks out on her own honeymoon before consummating her marriage in order to kill the Evil Queen who has threatened to harm the townspeople. Snow's loyalty to her husband, town, and father are evident that she has accepted the paternal law and would otherwise be perfectly inscribed within it, had there not been a malevolent female presence attempting to lure her to her own destruction through the use of knowledge that does not adhere to that paternal law. As Rozario (2004) notes, in many of the fairytales featuring an evil queen, the king/father figure is usually quietly done away with. Similar to the horror films discussed in the previous chapter, his absence is the precursor for the attempted destruction of his daughter. His ineffectiveness is ultimately what positions Snow as potentially regressing into the melancholic position. This is demonstrated in *Once*, when Snow's character, following the death of her father, and before meeting Prince Charming, is in a constant cycle of vengeance with the Evil Queen. In another scene,

Snow is given the chance to kill the Evil Queen's mother with magic, which she takes, and then succumbs to a deep depression, characterized by her heart beginning to turning black, like the Evil Queen's. Her desire for revenge rests on attempting to regain the lost mother, which she cannot escape until she meets her prince and forms a family. Similarly, Snow White in *The Huntsman* is a more active character than the Disney version. She is vengeful and portrayed as erring more on the androgynous or masculine side, with dirty skin and clothes and even dressed as a knight at one point. In contrast to the original story, the father is not absent, but rather murdered by Ravenna, which she justifies by claiming that men like him exploit the beauty of women and discard them. In contrast, later in the film, while Snow is in a coma, the Huntsman confesses his love for her, claiming that she reminded him of his dead wife. Snow then has two women with which she must navigate her relationship to. Ravenna is the woman who refuses to accept her lack, and therefore kills the man who reminds her of it, whereas the Huntsman's wife is pure lack, literally since she ceases to exist, and therefore cannot be for him what he lacks. This is similar to the Oedipal game for the young girl, where she must first identify with the woman who lacks if she is to assume the role of being what he lacks. By identifying with the mother-figure who refuses her own lack, the young girl will be unable to constitute the phallus in the other, suggesting he does not have what she needs. The cautionary tale is still available to girls and young women in this reiteration assuming the position of the one who has the phallus as a woman is indicative of evil.

Writer Angela Carter, known for her feminist, magical realism novels, and short stories, writes her own version of the Snow White tale in her book *The Chamber of Bloody Secrets* (1979), along with several other versions of fairytales. The story, "Snow-Child," is one of Carter's shortest, with only about 500 words. The story explains how a Count and Countess are out for a horseback ride in the middle of winter and as they ride, the Count begins to express his desire for a girl as white as snow, red as blood, and black as a bird's feathers. Upon his final lamentation, a girl appears with black hair, red lips, and snow white skin, naked by the side of the road. The Countess devises several ways to leave the girl behind or kill her, but the Count always intervenes, foiling each of the Countess's plans. With every attempt to harm the girl, one of the Countess's lavish garments, usually made out of an animal hide, leaves her body and wraps itself around the young girl, eventually leaving the Countess naked and the young girl adorned in furs. The Countess requests that the young girl pick her a rose, which the Count allows, as he sees no harm in this. The young girl picks the rose, pricks her finger, and dies. The Count jumps from his horse and defiles the corpse of the young girl, while the clothes are magically returned to the Countess. The child melts into the snow and the Count hands the rose to the Countess, to which she drops, proclaiming, "It bites!" (Carter, 1979, p. 92).

Carter, known for re-envisioning fairytales to reveal disturbing themes and morals, skews the popular story in order to demonstrate some of its more subtle elements, which can then be mined for their relevance to concerns about sexual difference and adolescent development. In this story, it is the man's desire which constitutes Snow, as she quite literally appears as the result of his yearning. This subversion of the traditional assumption regarding a maternal instinct also calls into question Oedipal desire on the part of the father. The clothes, of course, coming to represent the Countess slowly being replaced by the child, who, it seems may be on the precipice of becoming a woman herself, as noted in the allusions to the color of red contrasted against the white snow. The rape of the child's corpse is a vulgar depiction of this Oedipal desire, suggesting the violence women face at acquiescing to the paternal authority. Perhaps this is why the Countess simply "looks on narrowly" (p. 92), not from jealousy, but with indifference or boredom. However, it is also this disturbing scene that not only exposes some of the more insidious motifs of the children's story, but also develop a consideration of the ways in which young women come to identify with the femme fatale, albeit sometimes only in the transitory years of adolescence, in order to navigate the ways in which woman is symptom of man.

In each of these stories, whether it is the rather sanitized Disney version or Carter's horror story, Lacan's (1972) assertion that woman is the symptom of man is evident. This is literally the case, as these stories were penned by men and thus rely on a particular fantasy about female desire, but also in the fact that Snow always seems to be situated either directly or indirectly to the man's desire, whether it be her father or the Count, the prince who accosts her in a coma, or the dwarves who function as transitional father figures, and "know best." Zizek (1992) elaborates on Lacan's claim and states that "if woman is the symptom of man, the man himself can only exist through woman qua his symptom" (p. 177). This is perhaps the most apparent in Carter's short story, with the young girl manifesting following the Count's wishes. What Carter demonstrates in this story, however, is that a transition on the part of the child is needed in order for the man to permit himself to take her as a sexual object. Is this not also the case if we consider the trajectory from fairy tale to femme fatale, which, as I have argued seem to pivot on the role of the Evil Queen? The Evil Queen's, in all reiterations, attempt to possess that which they cannot, mainly, eternal life as evidenced by youth or beauty, but yet seem to have little use for the men in their lives. They are intensely powerful and beautiful, and yet their sexuality seems to be nonexistent, suggesting they literally have no use for the men in their lives. Carter's story illustrates this, as the Count is immediately possessed by that which his own lust created, and is thus dependent on. This seems to be a reversal of the femme fatale, whose cultivation of death runs contrary to immortality, and whose very existence (in film and in the plot) seems to rely on being seen and seducing men to do her bidding. As mentioned, the

Queen also does this, but the stories typically begin with the death of the father she has tricked into marrying her. The important distinction between the fairytales and the femme fatales is this relationship to death, with this compliance with death dictating the gaze of the spectator. The child in Carter's story is untouchable, but when pricked, and allusions to the loss of her chastity are intended here.

As I, and many others, have suggested earlier, fairytales serve as cautionary tales to young girls, and in this case, the Evil Queen is an example of who not to emulate. She is pure excess and it is her excess that leads to her own ruin. If Snow White and the Evil Queen are read as the same character, meaning that they represent the split within woman, the Evil Queen also represents a version of the death drive, bent on destroying her own virtue and ability to submit to castration. I will suggest that the femme fatale of the film noir genre, and contemporary films that employ similar tropes, function as the same sort of fairytale, but directed at a male audience, alerting them to the danger of their own desire qua woman. First, however, I would like to turn to another femme fatale figure outside of the film noir genre to explore the ways in which young women in particular come to identify with this split within themselves and cultivate a melancholic disposition. That is, the teen pop star.

The melancholic feminine of pop music

The melancholic female celebrity is one that many young women in particular are drawn to. While there are also male celebrities who also embrace a tragic sensibility, the female miserabilist is a stark contrast to the other ways female adolescence is represented, namely, cheerful, giddy, and an investment in brand name commodities. This contrast is playfully represented in the 1999 film *10 Things I Hate About You*, a modern spin on *The Taming of the Shrew*, in which one sister, Bianca, is a fan of models, pastels, and Prada backpacks, whereas Cat is shown reading *The Bell Jar*, a fan of Bikini Kill, and hoping to get accepted to Sarah Lawrence College. This disparity is perhaps the most prevalent in female musicians marketed to adolescent and young adult women. Though the face and voice changes, there seems to be a constant presence of the melancholic feminine whose music and appearance seems to conflate sexuality and death with inevitable despair. This particular portrayal of femininity perhaps serves as a transitory identification through which young women can come to reconcile with their lack, as well as a commodification with lack through which young women can re-enter contemporary culture and its emphasis on individual enjoyment.

There are several musicians, and actresses, across the decades that I could elaborate on. Artists like Janis Joplin, Nina Simone, and Edith Piaf all embodied femininity characterized by a certain melancholy, and were, and continue to be, transgressive women for the ways they challenged stereotypical gender norms about women. However, I would like to focus on a trend of musicians spanning the late 1990s and into the early 2000s, specifically artists such as Fiona Apple, Amy Lee, Jewel, Amy Winehouse, and Lana del Rey. These artists became popular alongside the boom in *Mickey Mouse Club* pop stars, which were singers who got their start on the popular children's show before transitioning into mega-stars, such as Britney Spears, Christina Aguilera, and members of the boy band N'sync. While the public watched with concern as teen idols turned into salacious young adults, baring their bellybuttons and grinding in music videos, young girls and women were turning to musicians with lyrics suggesting she has used a sensitive man and deserves to be punished for it. The accompanying video for Fiona Apple's "Criminal" featured a pale and sullen Fiona Apple undressing for a camera manned by a faceless man. Apple, among others, seemed to present a tragic form of femininity that ran contrary to the popular teeny boppers, exposing a certain sorrow latent in female sexuality.

Much of Fiona Apple's music focused either on lost love or being wronged, as was the case with Jewel, whose hits, "You Were Meant For Me" and "Foolish Games", are still popular among the lovelorn. Many of the music videos that accompanied the two singers' singles featured them usually looking sulkily at the camera, clothes falling off their thin shoulders, and rolling around on the floor or a bed. Their languidness became part of their persona. Amy Lee, of the band Evanescence, followed suit with haunting vocals, borderline gothic garb, and dark music videos. Similarly, her music revolved around heartache. What continues to stand out about these artists is the ways that their self-presentation emphasizes a dead-like quality. Pale, lethargic, and passive, their desire is dead. They have been enjoyed by a lover who has left them bereft. In contrast, Lana del Rey has been described as "gloomy pop" (Johnston, 2017), where she simultaneously mourns lost loves and the state of society, all while dressing up like Jackie O and Marilyn Monroe. Her music, as well as her style, suggests a pining, not for a lover, but for another time, assumedly the 1960s, a time she would not have been alive to see herself.

With each of these artists, there seems to be dead lover which they have come to orient around. Though Kristeva argued that it was a dead mother in which the melancholic could not get past, it is the dead mother who cannot take a new lover, and thus direct her desire elsewhere. Similarly, Soler (2003) suggests that feminine jouissance comes from the (non)presence of a dead lover, to which nothing can be offered up as a substitute. While Lana may also mourn past loves, her nostalgia for a time she never saw, also functions as a fantasy for the mother/lover that could have been —a time that would have satisfied her. Instead, she is forced to contend with the commodities and sensibilities she seems to find tedious. It is not fair to assume this is the actual circumstances of these women. They are products to be marketed as any other. Rather, I am interested in the ways in which this persona becomes a sort of layover for young women navigating their own desire and dead mother/lovers. In going through the Oedipus complex, the young girl must contend with both her own and her mother's lack, that is, what can never be. She must mourn the lover she will never have. Perhaps this is the reason that female adolescence is rife with stereotypes about mood swings, black clothing, and depressed music.

In this sense, the melancholic pop stars function as a sort of femme fatale in the sense that they are a repository for lack, thus providing a way in and, hopefully, through the suffering implicit in this discovery. They join the ranks of the many tortured beautiful souls that have come before them, with their songs serving as poetry, addressing a shared affect about a nameless lover, or a meaningless existence. What makes them particularly interesting in contemporary culture is that, like the Evil Queen in Snow White, there is juxtaposition between two types of feminine enjoyment. While the femme fatale of the pop world functions as a signifier for both depression and death, the teeny bopper endorses the masturbatory idiocy of phallic jouissance. Psychoanalyst Paola Mieli (1997) identifies the subject of the capitalist discourse as being "a subject … that never ceases being an idiot in producing enjoyment from exploitation" (p. 181), with idiot referring to a private person, removed from social responsibility. This masturbatory enjoyment in which capitalism thrives, refers to the retreat from the other as the source of desire and pleasure, with the assumption that such desire can be satiated within the self. As Soler (2003) notes, the depressive state is itself a mode of jouissance, but in contrast to a jouissance attempting to reclaim a lost object, the melancholic attempts "to speak herself as Other" (p. 105) because, as Lacan (1990) states, it is impossible for a woman to find a way of dealing with the unconscious completely. Soler understands this surplus of melancholy as intimately tied to the feminine lament for a dead lover.

To further lay out this contrast, consider two songs addressing a similar topic: Fiona Apple's "Not About Love" and Ariana Grande's "Thank you, next." Both songs are about a rejection of a previous lover. Grande claims to have found solace in not only moving from one man to the next, all of which she has claimed to learn something from, but has found true love in herself. In contrast, Apple's song seems to refer to a lack of a lack, claiming she misses the ache and as the title implies, it is not about love, but rather that she keeps falling out of love. While both songs were popular, Grande's song spent two weeks on the Billboard charts, something rare for a solo female artist to accomplish (Sisario, 2019). There seems to be a form of femininity in contemporary culture that is exalted in the media, which tends to correspond to capitalist sentiments. As Soler suggests, because of her ability to expose a certain reasonless to the world, the depressed person threatens the social bond. If we understand the contemporary social bond as predicated on an exchange of commodities and the promise of surplus enjoyment without the intrusion of the other, the melancholic further functions as a femme fatale, threatening to undo our stake in our own enjoyment. She demands an Other, who does not exist, to account for her suffering. However, similar to the Evil Queen in *Once*

Upon A Time, she too is matriculated into the system via her own signification. The melancholic pop star breaks into public sphere occasionally as an identification for those who may have not found purchase in the world of phallic jouissance, so that you can enjoy your depression, or evil side, without disturbing other's jouissance.

If woman is symptom of man, these two distinct manifestations of woman may also signify something about male desire and the question about sexual difference. While the examples I have previously discussed seem to demonstrate the ways in which a contention with lack and identification with the mother who lacks produces a surplus of melancholy that is reminiscent of the self-destructing tendencies of the femme fatales, there is always a way out that is offered up provided an exchange is made. This exchange could be jealousy and revenge in exchange for a desire for power and a title, or grief and melancholia in exchange for a song or persona through which to identify instead of the dead mother. However, the femme fatale is traditionally understood as a representation of male anxiety, as represented in the noire film genre. As I mentioned earlier, these films have been analyzed as a symptom of the socius, suggesting that male fear about the desire of women post World War II gave birth to the femme fatale. Following this assertion, I want to consider contemporary femme fatales, who though similar to their predecessors, seem to embody modern concerns about the state of the sexes. Though they find representation in neo-noir films, such as *Basic Instinct* (1992) and *Gone Girl* (2014), femme fatales also make their way into nontraditional genres, as is the case of *Inception* (2010) or *Under the Skin* (2013). These discourses then find traction within certain communities that identify the femme fatale as a true instantiation of the Woman, as opposed to understanding her as yet another symptom.

The woman who has it all

Much has been said about the femme fatale and her relationship to the male gaze. Such work tends to engage with sophisticated readings of psychoanalytic theory and film theory, with emphases on camera angles, lighting, and costume. Mary Ann Doane's (1991) excellent book covers many such themes, elucidating the relationship between visibility and truth that the femme fatale represents, as Beckman (2012) notes "an alluring secret that has to be revealed" (p. 25). As I have demonstrated in this book, and as others have done elsewhere, the dangerous woman is not a new figure and can be found throughout history in stories, plays, paintings, poetry, and film. The dangerous woman as sexually alluring suggests a concern about following one's desires too far. This is consistent with a Lacanian understanding of the subject, as the attainment of the actual object of desire would cause the subject to implode into itself with no recourse from the Other. Elizabeth Cowlie (1993) goes so far as to suggest that the term "femme fatale" is an epithet for sexual difference, with the femme fatale serving as a patriarchal tool on the warn against women who threaten male power.

While I do not entirely disagree with this trajectory of analysis, there seems to imply a certain conscious intention to subjugate femininity because of the threat it poses. This is a problem with many arguments about sexism and oppression against women within the feminist discourse. It suggests that men know what they do and do it anyway. This is of course the case in several circumstances. For example, a husband who physically abuses his wife may indeed have some unconscious reasons for doing so, but he also should be able to surmise that his behavior is criminal and contemptible. However, even in a case such as this, the locus of the man's subjectivity is assumed to be at the seat of conscious thought, meaning his ego. For those invested in psychoanalysis, this proposition is problematic. The attempts to represent particular types of women, though they can be certainly be considered reductionary and biased, must also be understood as an unconscious question about the desire of woman. Interpretations of the femme fatale as explicitly sexist also relies on a reading of the films as a literal representation between the sexes, and fails to consider the nonrapport, thus sticking perhaps a bit too close to the manifest content of the film to the exclusion of the fantasy. While Doane suggests that the femme fatale should also not be regarded as a feminist character, this ignores the fact that many women do in fact find themselves drawn to her as an empowering figure.

In order to demonstrate some of the nuances to the fantasy about sexual difference, from both sides of the matrix, an examination of some contemporary films that feature a femme fatale provide an opportunity to discuss the unconscious investment in such representations. The first one I consider, *Basic Instinct*, has been written about at length. However, within the context of sexual difference and the other films considered, the role of the fantasy about feminine desire becomes more explicit. The film follows Nick, played by Michael Douglas, a detective, who is drawn to Catherine, played by Sharon Stone, a woman he believes to have murdered her boyfriend. Catherine is wealthy, beautiful, hypersexual, and writes mystery novels that closely resemble the murders of her boyfriends. The recurring theme of dangerous sex or sex that could potentially end in the male protagonist's death is perhaps what this film is best known for. Several scenes depict Nick as either having difficulty restraining himself from Catherine or giving in to his urges despite an explicit fear that she may kill him. For example, when he asks her what her novel is about, she replies "A detective who falls in love with the wrong woman," to which he asks "What happens?" and she replies "She kills him." Despite his ongoing conviction that she is the murderer, Nick falls in love with Catherine, all the while worrying for his own safety. However, in the end it is discovered that Beth, another woman Nick is sleeping with, who is also his psychiatrist, is the murderer. Beth was in love with Catherine while in college, so much so that not only did she attempt to change her appearance to look like her, she also systematically killed Catherine's lovers.

In contrast, *Gone Girl* is not about a writer per se, though it does see a woman manipulating her own story to entrap a man. Amy, the subject of her parents' successful children's book series *Amazing Amy*, is happily married to Nick. On their fifth wedding anniversary, Amy goes missing, and the investigation reveals that Amy and Nick were having several problems, including an ongoing affair Nick was having with one of his students. It is revealed that Amy has staged her own abduction in the hopes that Nick would be blamed. However, when her own plan does not turn out and she returns, blaming an ex-boyfriend kidnapped her, who she murdered to escape. The ruse is discovered by Nick, but Amy convinces him to stay with her, which he does so reluctantly. While there is also dangerous sex portrayed in this film as well, as Amy murders the ex-boyfriend attempting to care for her just as he finishes copulating with her, there is not the same threat that Amy will kill Nick, as there was with Catherine and Nick.

It is perhaps a bit more explicit in *Gone Girl* that dangerous sex is a stand in for the sexual nonrapport in this masculine fantasy, though both films explicate different tangents of it. While castration anxiety may be an overt interpretation of these films, the issue in both films does not seem to be about castration but refusing the phallus as a stand in for being. Sex relies on what Lacan referred to as the masquerade, in which the feminine subject must assume the position as the one who lacks and invest in the mistaken assertion that the phallus of the other as the thing she lacks. In both films, she has "it" in all its instantiations, whether it be the literal phallus or its symbolic equivalents such as money or a career. The anxiety comes in the realization that whatever it is, may not be enough. For both Amy and Catherine, their sexual appetites seem insatiable and the men in their lives seem to offer up whatever they can in order to satisfy them to no avail. It is implicitly suggested that whatever it is that these women want, it will threaten to ruin these men's lives. If the woman is unable or refuses to constitute the phallus as that which she lacks, the man is once again unarmed against the jouissance of the other.

The addition of a same-sex love story in *Basic Instinct* seems to speak more to the hypersexualization of Catherine's character, as opposed to a turn toward a progressive script. There are several occasions in which Catherine has the opportunity to explain that she was not in love with her partners, and was only interested in having sex with them, shirking conventional gender roles and letting Nick know that she has sex like a man. Prior to the famous scene where she uncrosses her legs to expose her genitals, she claims "I have nothing to hide." This line in conjunction with Catherine exposing herself (i.e., lack), invites Nick into the masquerade, while also undermining his own investment by flaunting her female lover in front of him. She positions herself as having whatever the other lacks, while introducing a question about her own lack. In doing so, Catherine is in the position to both constitute Nick's phallus, as well as undermine its utility. His desire for and enjoyment of her is always subverted by potential for his own humiliation, castration, or death.

This contradiction is demonstrated from the beginning of the film, with Nick being introduced as a hot-headed detective and Catherine a wealthy mystery writer. His role is to pursue knowledge at all costs, while her job is to inscribe and evade knowledge, dancing around the truth but always evoking suspicion, like any good mystery novel is wont to do. It is interesting that Amy in *Gone Girl* is also the subject of works of fiction, though written by her parents as opposed to herself. Another film featuring a femme fatale, *Fatal Attraction*, also features the femme fatale, Alex, played by Glenn Close, as a book editor and working with Dan, a lawyer, also played by Michael Douglas. In each of these characterizations, the woman's connection with language is evidence of her dangerousness. These are not just career women, and thus positioned as not needing the man's phallus because they have their own, but rather that they are closer to a dangerous truth, the fallibility of the phallus. However, it is not just the fallibility of the phallus, but their position within and to language, both as women and writers (or in Amy's case, the revisionist) to upend the entire enterprise—whether that be a murder case and his redemption as a detective in *Basic Instinct*, the man's position within his family as in the case of *Fatal Attraction*, or his freedom, as in *Gone Girl*, in which it is Amy's return from her staged kidnapping that prevents her husband from leaving to be with his girlfriend. In each case, the threat is not of just castration, but that the fantasy that the presence of the woman's desire has the capability of jeopardizing of all jouissance on the part of the man. This becomes particularly crucial in considering Incel and MGTWO discourse later.

I have been considering these films from the assumption that they are a form of masculine fantasy. While I believe this to be true, to end the analysis there would be to once again to assume a conscious misogyny on the part of those writing these films or deriving pleasure for them. As I have suggested earlier, psychoanalysis offers a more nuanced perspective on the dynamics that could be labeled as sexist or misogynistic. Perhaps more than an arena in which to indulge a certain fantasy about the nature of the desire of women, such films also stage a complaint on the behalf of the masculine side of the sexual nonrapport. In this sense, the actual Woman remains elsewhere, which of course is echoed in the commonplace compliment "You're not like other women/girls." With such a statement, the man is trying to nominate this woman as the Woman, a phallic injunction that locates her immediately outside of the relationship between he and the Woman to which he now relates. Similarly, these films function as a complaint that splits woman/Woman. Catherine and Amy function within the film as fantasy as the Woman who seeks to undermine meaning and phallic investment, and the jouissance that comes with it. If fantasy, as Riggs (2015) suggests, "accords us a position from which we can reach the desire that is denied to us- it tells us where we need to be positioned in order to approximate the position of our first Other" (p. 17) than the femme fatale is as Woman allows for an escape from the seductive Other, with our dignity/phallus intact, while also indexing that imminent danger. It is a way of asserting "Look what I went through," begging witness to a certain suffering. As Miller (1991) states, analysis is a praxis grounded in suffering, with the articulation of a complaint to which the analyst must take on to effect the cure. The cure in psychoanalysis must be grounded in an ethics that allows for an apprehension of the symptom, though not necessarily the eradication of the symptom.

This does not quite answer what it is that women get out of such figures, however. In attempting to do so, Kaplan (1978) identifies the femme fatale as a figure of resistance, thus making her an alluring feminist icon. She suggests that film noir functioned as a fantasy for women as well, as it was a place that portrayed women as powerful and with sexual agency. The femme fatale also typically thwarts the male protagonist's desire and thus serves as a symbol of resistance to male domination. While this is likely the case to some extent, it still privileges conscious, even subconscious perhaps, identification with the image of the fantasy and finds within it a source of empowerment, meaning ego reifying. I wonder, however, if there is another desire latent in this identification that may expose the divided nature of woman, and thus returning the femme fatale to her position as a disturbing character for both sides of sexuation.

One of the more disturbing aspects of the femme fatale is that she seems to knowingly plunge forward to her own demise, disregarding the lifelines that are available to her. While she can be lauded for her feminist qualities for stymying the desire of the patriarchal figures, it is perhaps her own subjective division that allows for such a nihilistic identification. While all subjects are split subjects in the Lacanian framework, Soler (2003) claims that women must bear another split, which results in a fascination with the abyss of the Real. To demonstrate this, she returns to Lacan's (1972) comments on Paul Claudel's 1906 play *Break of Noon* in which he claims that he succeeded in creating a true woman in the character of Ysé. Ysé asks her husband to protect her from herself, and against the "horrible freedom" (p. 1184) she is afflicted with. Without going too much into the play itself, Ysé finds herself in three different affairs with men who all constitute different relationships to the object choice. Ysé herself, however, seems to be tempted by something beyond the phallic objects she surrounds herself with. This, according to Soler, is what leads Lacan to assert that she is a true woman, and it is the quality that is represented in the femme fatale, both in the classical film noir genre, and also in the melancholic pop stars, and evil queens. As Soler states, "she betrays all the objects that respond to the lack inscribed by the phallic function, and she does so to the profit of the abyss" (p. 18). The allure of the femme fatale to the woman may have more to do with a fantasy about an apprehension of one's own death drive and self-subverting qualities. As Lacan claimed in *Encore*, a woman has an unconscious only "from the place from which man sees her … (in which it) works in such a way that she knows nothing" (p. 90). Women, in the position of spectator, have a unique opportunity to occupy both a phallic and feminine position in relation to the femme fatale, which allows for objectification and empathy simultaneously.

The femme fatale and the men who hate them

Film allows for a representation of a fantasy in a way that coalesces in a contained plot. However, that fantasy, in this case, the fantasy about the desire and nature of the Woman, finds itself rearticulated in discourse as well. Before considering the potential for radical politics in the femme fatale, I would like to turn briefly to a contemporary social group that has been gaining more attention in North America: MGTOW's. MGTOW stands for "Men Going Their Own Way," which represents a group of men who claim to be removing themselves from heterosexual relationships. Their main contention is that contemporary heterosexual relationships are exploitative of men, largely due to feminism, and that the only way to combat this is by refusing to have relationships with women. The ones that do continue to have relationships with women claim to do so with women who assume a subservient role. These forums are typically filled with a collection of stories about times men have been wronged by women, misogynistic memes, and advice on how to handle women. There are also several YouTube channels and podcasts dedicated to helping men "go their own way," with advice ranging from how to train a woman to be subservient, to how to get over a heartbreak, to how to literally take care of oneself without a woman. A visit to these forums demonstrates an overwhelming number of stories, typically in the "Introductions" thread featuring men who have been hurt or abused by women or believe themselves to be unfairly disadvantaged by systems that favor women, such as the legal system in custody battles. These men openly share with one another, under screennames of course, respond to each other, and seem to offer support to one another. However, they also come up with derogatory terms and acronyms, none of which are suitable to reprint here, as well as an exposition of violent fantasies about the women in their lives.

Within the misogynistic rhetoric, there is a clear fantasy about what a woman is, what she wants, and how she will ruin a man to get it, "it" usually being money and children, which seem to refer to tropes reminiscent of the femme fatale. For example, one young man talks about living with an older woman who also happened to be his human resources representative at his job. He states that she was psychologically abusive, and when he retaliated by cheating on her, she threw him out and had him fired. When he sought out advice from a lawyer, he claims that the lawyer advised him not to, as men were not believed to be victims of abuse (Participant 11631, 2015). Another member claims that the following are things about women he knows to be true: "women are communists; women break whatever they get their hands on. Just the 'flow' of something will be broken by a woman; women will betray our bill of rights; women will get us all killed" (B4TOW, 2016). There are several other posts like this in which participants offer both their experiences and the things they know to be true about women, and several of them have this same conspiratorial tone. Regardless of personal circumstances, there seems to be a shared agreement that women's desire is inherently destructive to men, and those who do not share this perspective are said to be "blue pilled," a reference to the film *The Matrix* (1999), whereby taking the blue pill instead of the red pill is to remain in the fantasy and not see reality for what it truly is.

It is not my intention to psychoanalyze the participants of these forums, nor do I claim that this would be within my repertoire. However, the frequent invocations of the woman as manipulative, deceitful, and the cause of the destruction of man seem to rely on an assertion in response to a question about sexual difference. While the femme fatale may be a fictional character, the discourses surrounding her are taken up and mobilized in reaction to women. In each of these stories offered up by the men, the real woman is once again located elsewhere so that the Woman can be evoked. In doing so, the Other is chastised for wanting what the subject, in this case the MGTOW, while the man can retain his phallus. This allows the phallus to remain veiled. As McGowan (2018) explains, "the subject does not relate to the phallus, but must do so at the recognition of the Other's desire" (p. 15). The femme fatale character allows for a displacement that further veils the phallus, thus making it the signifier through which to make meaning. While it may appear that this misogynistic discourse is about women, it is actually about the men themselves. This is not to say that this form of discourse is not harmful and does not contribute to the oppression and abuse of women in patriarchal societies. However, in understanding that in inciting the Woman as a sort of femme fatale, the men in these groups can have their phallus constituted, especially during times when that may have been in question, such as in the case of the young man dating a HR representative, someone who had the authority to determine his position within a company.

Death and jouissance

It is useful to once more turn to Deleuze and Guattari's notion of becoming-woman here as a means to discuss the ways in which this particular type of monstrous woman is able to destabilize molarized identities. As I have argued, it seems that those women I have loosely identified as femme fatales are created as a means through which to explore anxiety about a woman's desire and jouissance. In doing so, the question of the significance of the phallus and the potential to open up onto a line of flight onto becoming-woman is possible. This is similar to the cases of feminine monsters that I have discussed throughout this book. However, the femme fatale offers a unique opportunity to discuss the role of subjective annihilation in jouissance and becoming-Other.

In many ways, the femme fatale is the ideal figure to locate an opportunity to consider becoming-Other. She is a split object for the spectator, who is both alluring and dangerous. The queens of the children's fables hold this same potential, especially for the young girls engaging with them. They are asked to notice the split within themselves and even momentarily, ask, what if? This what if ultimately corresponds to submitting to the Other within oneself. Using Deleuze's (1967) work on masochism, Studler (1985) argues that the femme fatale represents a mother figure that recalls the mother of infancy who does not lack, but rather possesses what the male child does not—the womb and the breast. She is alluring because of her plentitude, a plentitude that the child/spectator once had access to via the mouth-breast assemblage. Deleuze and Guattari (1980) suggest that an assemblage is when partial, heterogeneous objects connect to each other, sharing flows. In the mouth–breast assemblage, the desiring mouth receives the flow of milk from the breast and a new body is created, even momentarily. The problem is that as the infant becomes subjectivized, it becomes fixated into its molar identity and gradually loses the conscious awareness of the assemblages it could be creating. However, this does not mean that the plentitude of the Other within oneself is out of limits of unconscious reach. The Other of the unconscious is the same Other that Lacan theorized we formulate symptoms in response to. By understanding that the Other as a source of surplus flows and intensities, they suggest a radical breaking from the habitual response to the presence of the Other that attempts to preserve subjectivity, and instead enter into an assemblage with the Other.

However, it also important to once again take seriously Braidotti's (2011) concern regarding shedding identities in hostile contexts and the project of becoming-woman for those who may have less than a foot in the Symbolic order to begin with. Becoming-woman may be the first step toward alterity, but for those that are already in the position of being other, it is not clear what further deterritorialization may need to occur, or how to avoid those attempting to violently reinscribe those in the position of the other into phallic discourse. The femme fatale, as a figure of not only sensuality and power, but also coldness and ambivalence, offers a line of flight for those bodies and subjectivities overdetermined with injunctions to be feminine or female. Initially, this coldness and ambivalence registers as cruelty and as spectators of films with a femme fatale, we respond with suspicion or fear. This has more to do with the habitual responses to the body that has been territorialized as female then it does with the actual desire of the woman in question. In many ways, then, this encounter with a femme fatale is a sort of death because it is a death of what we have come to know, especially in relation to the Other, and just as in the case with the mothers I discussed in an earlier chapter, it may mean coming to terms with an Other that is now entirely made alien.

This alienness is what allows for the counteractualization of the female body and discourses that seek to territorialize feminine subjects. For the feminine subject, attempting to become-other means acknowledging subjective death inherent to one's gender notions and ideals. As Massumi (1992) explains,

> one can only come to one's assigned cliché. Like metal to a magnet that recedes farther into the distance from the closer one draws, in an endless deflection from invention. The only end is death. Gender is a fatal detour from desire-in-deviation (every body's secret potential and birthright) ... Gender is a form of imprisonment, a socially functional limitation of a body's connective and transformational capacity.
> (p. 87)

As spectators of the femme fatale, we are reminded of encroaching death in the form of servitude or phallic dominance, whether it be the detective who is attempting to catch her in the act, or the various forces attempting to reign in the Queen's power. Her desire is what mobilizes her and specifically why she is unable to simply behave as deemed necessary by those wielding the law. As Massumi goes on to say, "as long as there is familial overcoding, there will be a need for gender politics to defend and empower those disfavored by the exercise in containment that is molar Man ... Breaking in is an enabling strategy for breaking away" (p. 88). The femme fatale, whether she be the evil queen, a Sharon Stone character, or the strawwomen erected in the discourses of groups such as MGTOW, utilizes the oedipal overcoding that renders her always already m(O)ther, and uses it to chip away at the signification of the phallus, and thus molar identity.

This potential of the femme fatale is particularly realized when the distinct lack of femme fatales represented in the media is considered. This is not to say that there are not representations of women who murder or manipulate. Films like *Kill Bill* (2003) or *The Girl with the Dragon Tattoo* (2011) feature exceptionally violent women. Shows like *Gossip Girl* and *Pretty Little Liars* are some of the closest iterations of the femme fatale, with each show portraying an omniscient, anonymous female character who pulls the strings of socialites to produce drama, intrigue, and violence. Many other representations, such as in the case of *Black Swan* or *Side Effects* seem to rely on tropes of mental illness, and thus further territorialize aberrant behaviors as pathological. Similarly, movies such as *Fatal*

Attraction and *Basic Instinct* have been subject to clinical evaluations, with Alex Forrest being understood as having borderline personality disorder, and Catherine Tramell with antisocial personality disorder.

However, what is different from these contemporary representations that are consistent in the earlier depictions of femme fatales is a distinct lack of desperation on the part of the woman in question. They are vengeful, mentally ill, or merely just power hungry, but they do not seem to express a notable desperation to flee their various contingencies. In essence, the contemporary femme fatale is predominantly masculine, though feminized via feminine tropes, such as gossipy, passive aggressive, and hypersexual. This is particularly important in the contemporary moment. From a Lacanian and Deleuzian perspective, the American feminist movement is problematic because of its aspirations to be more fully accounted for within the Symbolic order, which has come to mean significations of wealth and power. This is problematic because neoliberal capitalism seeks to interpolate more individual bodies into its fold, flattening difference in the name of the dollar sign. Furthermore, the hyperphallic femme fatale does not illicit anxiety in the same way. She is easily known because her desire is predicated on phallic jouissance—that is, she always wants what the other has. In contrast, the disturbing aspect of some of the earlier femme fatales is specifically that she wants what the other does not have, and therefore there is nothing to brace against her jouissance. The contemporary version of femme fatale is intentional in her manipulation and concerned with being (powerful, successful, wife, etc.) and forecloses upon becoming. She is not only knowable, but she is marketable. Her desire is a closed loop, not excessive, but directed at a thing she can attain.

The femme fatales I have discussed here and those of film noir open onto becoming specifically because her desire leads her into opportunities for creativity. It is not just that she manipulates the man in question, but rather she continually asks what she and he can do together. She accepts her fate as directional, but not intentional with her desire, while he attempts to stave off her jouissance with knowledge. Central to her fate is the impending death, which as I have mentioned, is not necessarily literal death but the death of this knowledge wielded to confine her desire. Her desire moves her into paths of becoming-Other, which will always appear as death as she must leave behind remnants of a corpse. The corpse is the signification, in this case what constitutes a woman, that the nomadic subject must relinquish on her travels through hostile territory.

References

B4TOW. (2016, July 5). Greetings brothers [online forum post]. Retrieved from www.mgtow.com/forums/topic/greetings-brothers/

Beckman, F. (2012). From irony to narrative crisis: Reconsidering the femme fatale in the films of David Lynch. *Cinema Journal, 52*(1), 25–44.

Braidotti, R. (2011). *Nomadic subjects: Embodiment and sexual difference in contemporary feminist theory*. New York: Columbia University Press.
Carter, A. (1979). *The bloody chamber*. London: Victor Gollancz Ltd.
Cowlie, E. (1993). Film noir and women. In J. Copgec's (Ed.) *Shades of noir* (121–166). London: Verso Books.
Deleuze, G. (1967). *Masochism: Coldness and cruelty & venus in furs*. New York: Zone Books.
Deleuze, G. and Guattari, F. (1980). *A thousand plateaus: Capitalism and schizophrenia*. Minneapolis: University of Minnesota Press.
do Rozario, R.A.C. (2004). The princess and the magic kingdom: Beyond nostalgia, the function of Disney princess. *Women's Studies in Communication*, 27(1), 34–59.
Doane, M.A. (1991). *Femme fatales: Feminism film theory, psychoanalysis*. New York: Routledge.
Fincer, D., Director. (2011). *The girl with the dragon tattoo* [Film]. Columbia Pictures.
Glazier, J., Director. (2013). *Under the skin* [Film]. Studio Canal.
Jancovich, M. (2008). Female monsters: Horror, the 'femme fatale' and World War II. *European Journal of American Culture*, 27(2), 133–149.
Johnson, S. (2009, February 27). Whatever happened to the femme fatale? *The Independent*. Retrieved from https://web.archive.org/web/20090228103849/http://www.independent.co.uk/arts-entertainment/films/features/whatever-happened-to-the-femme-fatale-1633088.html (Accessed July 2 2019 and March 10 2020).
Johnston, M. (2017, July 25). Lana del Ray, *Lust for life*. *Rock's Backpages*. Retrieved from https://www.rocksbackpages.com/Library/Article/lana-del-rey-ilust-for-lifei (Accessed July 2 2019 and March 10 2020).
Kaplan, E.A. (1978). *Women in film noir*. London: British Film Institute.
Kitsis, E. and Horowitz, A. (2011–2018). *Once upon a time*. New York: ABC Studios.
Kristeva, J. (1982). *Powers of horror: An essay on abjection*. New York: Columbia University Press.
Kristeva, J. (1992). *Black sun: Depression and melancholia*. New York: Columbia University Press.
Lacan, J. (1972). *The seminar of Jacques Lacan: On feminine sexuality, the limits of love and knowledge (Encore)*. New York: W.W. Norton & Co.
Lacan, J. (1990). *Television: A challenge to the psychoanalytic establishment*. New York: W.W. Norton & Co.
Marshall, A., Producer. and Verhoeven, P., Director. (1992). *Basic instinct*. Los Angeles: Tristar Pictures.
Massumi, B. (1992). *A user's guide to capitalism and schizophrenia: Deviations from Deleuze and Guattari*. Cambridge: The MIT Press.
McGowan, T. (2018). The signification of the phallus. In S. Vanhuele, D. Hook, and C. Neil (Eds.), *Reading Lacan's ecrits: From 'signification of the phallus' to 'metaphor of the subject* (1–20). New York: Routledge.
Mieli, P. (1997). Brief preliminary considerations on sameness, otherness, idiocy, and transformation. In J. Houis, P. Mieli, and M. Stafford (Eds.), *Being human: The technological extensions of the body* (163–188). New York: Après-Coup.
Milchen, A., Donen, J., Witherspoon, R., Chaffin, C., Producers. and Fincher, D. (2014). *Gone girl*. Los Angeles: 20th Century Fox.
Miller, J.A. (1991). Ethics in psychoanalysis. *Lacanian Ink*, 5, 13–27.

Nolan, C., Director. (2010). *Inception* [Film]. Legendary Pictures.
Participant 11631. (2015, November 30). Re: I don't know [Online forum comment]. Retrieved from www.mgtow.com/forums/topic/i-dont-know/
Riggs, D.W. (2015). *Pink herrings: Fantasy, object and sexual difference*. London: Routledge.
Roth, J., Mercer, S., Producers. and Sanders, R., Director. (2012). *Snow White and the Huntsman*. Los Angeles: Universal Pictures.
Sanders, R. Director. (2012). *Snow white and the huntsman*. [Film]. Universal Pictures.
Sisario, B. (2019, February 25). Ariana Grande's 'Thank You, Next' repeats at no. 1. *The New York Times*. Retrieved from https://www.nytimes.com/2019/02/25/arts/music/ariana-grande-thank-u-next-billboard-chart.html (Accessed July 2 2019 and March 3 2020).
Sobchak, V. (1998). 'Lounge time': Post-war crisis and the chronotype of film noir. In N. Browne (Ed.), *Refiguring American film genres: History and theory* (129–170). Berkeley: University of California Press.
Soler, C. (2003). *What Lacan said about women: A psychoanalytic study*. New York: Other.
Studler, G. (1985). Masochism and the perverse pleasure of the cinema. In B. Nichols (Ed.), *Movies and methods volume II: An anthology* (602–625). Berkeley: University of California Press.
Tarantino, Q., Director. (2003). *Kill Bill: Vol 1* [Film]. Miramax.
Wachowski, L. and Wachowski, L., Directors. (1999). *The matrix* [Film]. Warner Bros.
Zizek, S. (1992). *Enjoy your symptom! Jacques Lacan in Hollywood and out*. New York: Routledge.

Chapter 7

The borderline, jouissance, and capitalist enjoyment

> A continual tug-of-war develops between the wish to merge and be taken care of, on the one hand, and the fear of engulfment, on the other.
> (Jerold K. Kreisman, *I hate you, don't leave me! Understanding the borderline personality*)

> I won't be ignored, Dan.
> (Alex Forrest, *Fatal attraction*)

In each of the previous chapters, I have discussed the ways in which a question about what constitutes sexual difference and the assumptions about a woman's desire can provoke an anxiety characterized by an inability to account for this sexual difference within the realm of language and signification. In this chapter, I would like to further my analysis on the contemporary sociohistorical moment in neoliberal, capitalist Western society that I began toward the end of the last chapter. In doing so, I would like to consider the ways in which these neoliberal capitalist discourses, in attempting to account perfectly for sexuality and sexed identities, create a specific type of feminine monster: the borderline. The Borderline, as opposed to borderline personality disorder (BPD), is the subject within the diagnosis. In contrast to a person who has depression or who gets anxious, the borderline embodies her diagnosis, and rather than having a personality disorder, she is a subject caught in between. Traditionally, this "in-between" referred to a subject who straddles neurosis and psychosis, making a definitive diagnosis difficult for the analyst. However, I would like to argue that the in-between that the borderline inhabits is the signification of Woman and the Woman in the Lacanian sense, which, I have attempted to argue, has been the case for several feminine subjects deemed monstrous. The borderline's threat is exacerbated in late-stage neoliberal capitalism because her surplus jouissance threatens to undermine perverse capitalist discourses premised in an imaginary surplus, which attempts to conceal castration in exchange for commodities and signifiers.

Borderline personality disorder

BPD—borderline personality disorder—is a psychiatric disorder, characterized by the *Diagnosis and Statistical Manual of Mental Disorders (DSM) 5* (2013) as a personality that is marked by instability. This instability manifests in impulsivity and disturbances of both the self and relationships. The person with BPD tends to remark that they experience feelings of emptiness, and are possessed with fears of abandonment, which leads to relationship valuations characterized by idealization and devaluation. The person with BPD may also engage in suicidal gestures and impulsive behaviors that are considered self-damaging, such as sex, substance abuse, and gambling.

While the National Institute of Mental Health is reporting that there is no gender or racial bias in the epidemiology of BPD, the American Psychiatric Association (2000) was claiming a 3:1 ratio for diagnosis in women up until the most recent publication of the *DSM*. Researchers claim that earlier reports of gender bias may be the result of clinicians' biases, rather than a gender bias inherent in the criteria for the disorder (Sansome and Sansome, 2011). Sansome and Sansome (2011) do also suggest that men are more likely to be diagnosed with a substance abuse disorder or antisocial personality disorder than woman and less likely than women to be diagnosed with BPD. Despite claims of gender neutrality made by the APA, research such as the aforementioned study by Sansome and Sansome (2011) suggest that there are particular symptoms that can be expected from women patients, that are either not present as frequently in males, or are not cause for concern when demonstrated by males, and therefore not considered symptomatic. Furthermore, the claim that the previous gender bias was caused by clinician bias does not merit a dismissal of previous statistics on demographics, as we cannot assume that clinicians have overcome this bias in the last four years, as it is the clinicians who are creating and interpreting the criteria, as opposed to the criteria being an objective truth that can be utilized without the intervention of a human third party. It is also important to consider that the *DSM* is written collaboratively by clinicians and researchers, and because clinician bias is claimed, bias is not automatically excluded from the text itself. Finally, it is worth noting that the *DSM*, nor the clinicians, and their patients exist outside of a culture that not only perpetually represents the borderline personality as distinctly feminine, but that it also prospers financially to do so, as suggested in the myriad recapitulation of the femme fatale motif in film and literature.

The term "borderline" was actually coined by psychoanalyst Adolph Stern in 1938, and, as mentioned, was used to designate an individual who was seen as being not quite neurotic or psychotic, and thus, inhabiting the borders of both. Lacan, however, claimed that there was no such subjective structure as "borderline" and that the only person who was caught between a neurotic and psychotic diagnosis was the analyst (Drob, 2008). One of the reasons for this is because the psychoanalytic interpretation of borderline symptomology has been to understand it as a failure in the development or regulation of the ego, which Lacan has little interest in (Drob, 2008). However, I am not concerned with the actual subjective structure of the person diagnosed with borderline personality, as much as I am interested in the ways in which the borderline has become a modern feminine monster through Lacan's theory of sexuation, as opposed to his approach to diagnostics.

I have argued elsewhere that there is an implicit gender bias in the symptomology of BPD (Morris, 2018), in which behaviors are especially considered excessive or impulsive when exhibited by women because they challenge assumed gender norms. Furthermore, characterizations of women with BPD in film and television cannot be separated from the discourses of psychiatry and psychology, as popular media and psychology have come to inform one another to the point it is almost impossible to objectively separate them. Films like *Fatal Attraction* exemplify not only the symptoms of BPD, such as impulsive, promiscuous, and engaging in self-harming behaviors, but also the demographic most likely to be diagnosed, which are single women who are independent, intelligent, and overtly sexual. Feminist scholars have argued that the term "borderline" has come to function in much the same way that hysteria did, in that it identifies pathology in women, without always accounting for the sociohistorical contingencies that produce certain behaviors (Jimenez, 1997; Wirth-Cauchon, 2001). The result then is not only a diagnostic category, but also a whole array of discourses that construct the borderline women as a particular type of dangerous woman, which becomes even more threatening when this too does not perfectly account for the woman. The specific danger that these subjects pose, I argue, is their ability to assume the position of the abject, which challenges capitalist and neoliberal discourses about subjectivity.

Psychiatry and neoliberal capitalism

Before explicating the ways in which the borderline subject could be understood as identifying with the abject, a consideration of the ways in which psychiatric discourses and neoliberal capitalism operate with one another is important. Of particular importance is the medicalization of suffering and neoliberal injunctions to efface the inability to solve the sexual relation and thus enjoy perfectly. The medicalization of suffering and psychiatry's relationship with neoliberal capitalism has been written about at length, whether it be the profits made by doctors and pharmaceutical representatives for prescribing and marketing medications to alleviate regular suffering, such as grief, or the ways in which the diagnostic categories represent neoliberal capitalist values of accumulation and productivity. Sugarman (2015) argues that in fact, psychological theories and practices actually contribute to and sustain neoliberal capitalism and calls for an ethics of psychology that seriously considers this collusion.

Earlier I explained how philosopher Michel Foucault analyzed the ways in which the production of knowledge became relegated to the medical establishment. Foucault (1973, 2006, 2008) also spent a great deal of time discussing the ways in which madness became medicalized. Psychiatry, as a medical discipline, came to enact its own juridico-discursive regimes, which produced knowledge that sought to explain and control the mad person and behavior deemed abnormal. Foucault (2008) argues that the shift from locking the mad person up in shackles and asylums to studying him and making him a subject of psychiatry essentially transitions from a system of violence to a microphysics of power. Rather than having simply his body incarcerated, the mad person's behaviors, thoughts, and feelings fell under the control of the psychiatrist. In the same text, he demonstrates how the Psy-complex came to exist, meaning those professions that deal with the psyche, and became a disciplinary power, with consciousness, and the unconscious, being subjected to moral injunctions, demands, and surveillance by doctors, nurses, government officials, and eventually, the person himself. The result is that the person comes to internalize the Psy-complex, governing their behaviors and thoughts and subjecting them to evaluation, and modifying them if they are assessed as deviant.

The role of the Psy-complex, and psychiatry in particular has become even more insidious since the time Foucault was writing. Psychiatrists and psychologists working with pharmaceutical companies are incentivized for not only diagnosing more and more people with mental disorders, but also for prescribing various psychotropic medications as treatment (Kirsch, 2011). Despite the fact that the APA has publicly stated that they have no empirical evidence for their assumption that a chemical imbalance causes mental disorders (Deacon, 2013), physicians and psychologists routinely prescribe antidepressants and antipsychotics, receiving monetary rewards for doing so (Kirsch, 2011). Skott-Myhre (2016) suggests that the effect is then that as more and more people identify the psychiatry business as lucrative, more and more people are able to be interpolated as abnormal, deviant, or sick.

In fact, it could be argued that psychiatry and capitalism reflect the same ideology, both of which thrive on individualism, and in particular, contemporary neoliberalism. U'Ren (1997) even suggests that the dominant tenets of capitalism are implicitly reflected in the assumptions and practices of psychiatry. Both capitalism and psychiatry rely on the individual acknowledging himself or herself as the locus of the problem, and that one of the essential problems of the mentally disordered person is their inability to participate in the economic system. This is explicitly stated in the *DSM* criterion B for all disorders, that the symptoms demonstrated must have an impact on the person's ability to work and have interpersonal relationships. Though work and interpersonal relationships may indeed be a large part of a person's identity and well-being, the issue is that the moral injunctions implicit in both capitalism and psychiatry are obscured by an emphasis on individual achievement, health, and success. As U'Ren explains, both capitalism and psychiatry place high value on work and productivity, with the responsibility of doing so on the part of the individual as part of their overall mental health. The individual who is unable or refuses to comply is expected, and sometimes forced, to consult a psychiatrist, who is inscribed within a system that sells mental health and well-being as a commodity. U'Ren goes on further to say,

> Capitalist society has brought into existence a class of experts trained to deal with the negative consequences of the very conditions that, historically, capitalism itself has helped bring about: disruption of local community life and emotional bonds, deracination, depersonalization of work, the anomie of urban life. Psychiatry and psychotherapy represent modes of treatment that eve evolved not only to provide relief of symptoms, but also to bring comfort encouragement and personal attention to lonely and demoralized individuals in a society where close personal relationships and community are often absent. However, the form of care is not the same for all social classes. Like all goods and services, care is distributed unevenly in a capitalist society depending upon ability to pay. The upper strata, at least until recently, have received therapy that is oriented toward insight and understanding, while those in the lower socio-economic strata get treatment that more closely resembles administrative management: hospitalization, briefer more directive psychotherapy and tranquilizing medications.
>
> (1997, p. 6)

The question that I would like to consider is how different disorders function to pathologize certain behaviors as a means to further obscure these implicit capitalist ethics, and more specifically, how do manifestations of sexual difference become interpolated into the capitalist psychiatric project. In doing so, I would like to suggest that subjects who reject phallic symbolization, and thus commodification, and are subsequently pathologized are those behaviors that may offer opportunities for challenging neoliberal capitalist subjectivity.

Borderline subjectivity and abjection

In order to consider the borderline and abjection, as mentioned earlier, I would like to propose thinking about borderline subjectivity, as opposed to a person with BPD. Such an approach deviates slightly from the Lacanian perspective, in that the borderline is not caught between hysteria and psychosis, but rather the feminine subject caught between the Symbolic and the

Real. As Hicks (1991) states, a border requires a border machine and patrol agents to control and inspect derived territories. These territories of self and other, similar to territories comprised by regimes of power and domination, rely on recognized cuts and gaps, which are frequently challenged and undermined. Borderline subjectivity is constituted by what it is not, by what it brushes up against, and also by what rejects it or refuses to account for it. Subsequently, borderline subjectivity is the site of surveillance. Similar to the subjects discussed in the previous chapters, the issue is not necessarily with the women as much as an issue with the ways in which the woman as Other challenges or transgresses phallic organization. Symptoms, then, are problematic not because they are inherently pathological or maladaptive, but because they demonstrate an inability to constitute the phallus of the other person, challenging their subjectivity by eliciting revulsion and thus effacing the borders that demarcate I/Other.

The symptom which is probably the most immediately disturbing to people is that of self-harming behavior. Self-harming behavior can manifest in a variety of ways such as cutting the skin, wrist banging and/or the consumption of harmful substances for the purposes of poisoning. These behaviors are not for the purposes of suicide, as many people who commit self-harm note that they have no interest in taking their own life (Strong, 1998). I am not as interested in the reasoning behind the behaviors as I am in the effect that they produce in the onlooker. In many cases, this is a signal that the person needs psychiatric attention demonstrated in the clichéd analysis that self-harm is a cry for help. Though I do not disagree, it must also be considered as an act that demands a response from the other and in doing so provokes anxiety in the other. However, the reason why the other's anxiety provokes him or her to act can be analyzed, especially considering some of the discourse surrounding self-harm. The aforementioned "a cry for help" is related to the explanation that the person is self-harming for attention, an evaluation made usually with a tone of derision or pity. The assumption being that the person engages in self-harm as a means to elicit sympathy and concern from another person, and yet, this alone does not seem to account for why the behavior is so offensive, or why eliciting sympathy is so threatening.

Self-harming behaviors, especially those made visible on the body, run the risk of threatening the I/other distinction. From a Lacanian perspective, the skin is an envelope that one comes to identify as the site of separation between the self and others, especially the Other. It is both a form of protection, as well as the site of subjective constitution. Considering the overrepresentation of women who are diagnosed with BPD and who self-harm, it becomes particularly relevant that people who self-harm remark that they feel drawn to cutting, as if it was a compulsion rather than a conscious decision to ask for help or attention (Strong, 1998). If the skin is an envelope, this compulsion can be understood as a desire to act on the border between self and other, and its violence is commensurate with the unconscious violence of the Other's jouissance. Kristeva (1982) remarks that the inside of the body, in this case, the blood on the skin, makes its presence to compensate for the intrusion of the Other and the collapse of the border between inside and outside. The issue, however, in the case of the person who self-harms, is that they identify with the abject. Kristeva argues further that transforming the abject into the site of the Other, gratifies the desire for the abject that subtantiates the symbolic authority of the phallic law.

The implications of this for the self-harming borderline woman is that her behavior is inherently seductive and that it marks her body as the site of the Other's jouissance while adhering to a paternal metaphor.

To put it another way, if we think about the self and Other through the metaphor of the host-virus plot that has become quite popular in horror films, the skin is the first line of defense against the virus (Other) as well as the screen upon which the first manifestations of infection are displayed. The person who enacts violence against this barrier, not only threatens their own subjectivity, but also potentially anyone who meets them, via an awareness of the presence of the Other in the unconscious, and yet there is a powerful draw to bring their body under the symbolic function through diagnosis and cure, which reinforces the authority of the symbolic function.

Another symptom to consider from this perspective is "identity disturbance." Psychoanalyst Otto Kernberg suggested that the difference between the neurotic person and the borderline person is that the borderline person is not able to provide a coherent description of themselves (Wirth-Cauchon, 2001). He also remarked that a characteristic of this identity disturbance is splitting, in which the person holds two contradictory perspectives of themselves and others and is unable to integrate them. The clinical literature reports similar experiences, stating that individuals tend to remark confusion at changes in their selves despite also noting polarized self-conceptions and a weak correspondence with reality (Gold and Kyratsous, 2017). However, as Wirth-Cauchon notes, countertransference plays a prominent role in the complicated relationship between the borderline and therapist. Many therapists and clinicians remark about the difficulty in treating borderline patients, attributing it to the patient's inconsistencies and contradictory behavior, as well as their tendency to be highly seductive. Wirth-Cauchon identifies this relationship as a struggle over boundaries, with the borderline refusing to remain in the patient role and instead trying to enter the therapist's life. I would like to suggest that rather than refusing to remain a patient and becoming too personal with the therapist, the borderline's inability to remain in a certain symbolic configuration then challenges the ways in which the therapist as other can interact with her based on what the therapist believes his or her own identity as therapist to be. The effect is that the borderline is unable to constitute the phallus, refusing to recognize the therapist, or friend, partner, etc., in the identity he or she has misunderstood themselves for. Schwartz-Salant (1987) remarks that the therapist,

> Amidst the emotional assaults he may feel- intense experiences that may result in temporary loss of his sense of identity, wholeness, and Eros- he may also tend to feel that the borderline person knows something. At first experienced as a vague uneasiness, this feeling makes him think he did err or somehow did harm. The patient may be totally unable to verbalize this, instead assaulting the therapist with an unpleasant energy field. The therapist becomes subject to the patient's scanning, a kind of imaginal sights that is peculiarly discomforting. [Her] sight is like the Negative Eye Goddess... in ancient Egypt, who roamed the waters before creation, destroying everything she saw.
>
> (p. 117)

Schwartz-Salant aptly articulates an attitude and fear some therapists have toward their borderline patients. The "something" the borderline knows in relation to the therapist's "temporary" loss of wholeness and Eros—of course, from a Lacanian orientation—is that he castrated, and his posturing as "therapist" is a façade premised in the other also misrecognizing him or her as an unbarred subject. The "energy field" as the result of the patient's failure to verbalize the experience is not something she emits, but something she elicits in her inability or refusal to participate in the phallic exchange. It is curious that the next sentence that follows this insight is that "the therapist becomes subject" though meaning "becomes subjected to," with the perhaps unintended implication that the therapist becomes (is reminded he or she is) a subject, meaning that he or she is castrated once more in the presence of the gaze of the Other occupying the place of the borderline, who "roamed ... before creation." Implicit in this is that the borderline in the place of the Other, in refusing to acknowledge the authority of the therapist and the boundaries that that signifier constitutes, rejects the phallus as offered to her by the therapist, which throws him or her into a state of anxiety in the realization that, the Other does not want the piece as the stand in for the whole.

This is not to say that the person in the therapist role actually experiences complete annihilation or ventures into psychosis. Rather, his or her grounding in the Psy-complex with its prominent signifiers allows him or her to couch the anxiety in therapeutic discourse, thus projecting that anxiety back onto the borderline subject. This allows the therapist to proceed without acknowledging that in those encounters, he or she had actually become the borderline subject, caught between the neurotic compromise and the induced psychosis brought on by the rejection of the phallus by the Other. It is this effect that I will first discuss of Deleuze and Guattari's idea of liminal spaces, and Ettinger's theory of borderlinking in relation to borderline subjectivity.

Liminal spaces and borderlinking

Borders and borderlines offer the opportunity to discuss liminal spaces as the site of creative production, which I would like to argue, has political potential in challenging the neoliberal capitalist production of subjectivity. In doing so, it is my intention to follow the work of Skott-Myhre (2014), which argues that the unconscious and desire are the site of revolutionary potential. However, I would like to deviate slightly and identify the borderline subject as our contemporary moment's instantiation of sexual difference, and thus a locus for the reorganization of the relationship to the phallus and subjectivity through the discomfort and abjection that she provokes.

Liminal spaces are gaps in signification in which the Real can intrude. For Deleuze and Guattari, liminal spaces are the spaces of pure force in which life itself exists, without the overcoding of capitalism, the Oedipus complex, etc. They suggest that one way to combat systems of signification and symbolization is to open up more liminal spaces, in which "the flow of creativity ... exceed the capacity of language" (Skott-Myhre, Pacini-Ketchabaw and Skott-Myhre, 2016). Victor Turner (as cited in Malone, 2000) furthers this claim, explaining that liminal spaces operate as a noncategorical between space that is both generative and inherent to the social tie. Malone (2016) explains that Lacan also works within liminal spaces, identifying moments when speech breaks down, not as a means to provide new speech, "but to render a crossing, a moment wherein speech and the Real crisscross fleetingly" (p. 197). In Lacanian theory, there are instances in which this liminality between language and the Real is accentuated, specifically in regard to the psychosis and femininity, in which as Malone puts it "is not a realm of understanding yet it does incarnate a liminiality, which allows the flash that only has a before and after" (p. 200). Thinking about those generative moments in liminal spaces as intrusions of the Real not only maintains the creative potential, but also the disturbing quality of pure alterity, which challenges any sort of romanticized fantasies about subjective experimentation.

One way of thinking through the potential in these liminal spaces is to return to Bracha Ettinger's theory of the matrixial borderspace. Within this theory, she proposes the "borderlinking," which has potential for the borderline subject. As I mentioned in the previous chapter, Ettinger conceived of the matrixial borderspace as a supplementary perspective to the Lacanian phallic unconscious, which allows her to think of subjectivity as constituted through an encounter. As Butler (2006) explains, subjects, at an unconscious level, prior to subjectification, are left in pieces, which can be linked together, but cannot properly bound the affect of historical losses and trauma. The matrixial stratum of the unconscious can be conceived of as the co-emergence of partial subjects, and borderlinking as the work one can do to respect the encounter. Ettinger argues that this can be done through art, though she also advocates for "ethical and political relations between strange, foreign, irreducible elements of otherness in our encounters with human and even nonhuman events in the world" (Pollack, 2006, p. 3). This borderlinking challenges Lacan's Real as beyond sense, and instead moves into a more Deleuzian understanding of the Real as a space in which subject to subject encounters can occur, even if nothing can be said about them, with the effect being inherently creative. Though the encounter with borderline subjects may not always be described as creative, the fact that they typically evoke anxiety, and trouble their therapists tends to mean that the traditional interventions fail to cause an effect. That is, the meaning that has functioned up to this point no longer corresponds to the object, and thus something else must arise as a result. Though Ettinger argues for an ethical and political relation with the strange and irreducible, phallic logic tends to exert force and violence, which cuts, castrates, and dichotomizes.

This tendency for therapists and others to be disturbed by borderlines, not to mention the tendency for individuals to refer to any difficult women they may have encountered as borderline, is an encounter that enacts a pre-Oedipal stratum of subjectivity. Though it may be anxiety provoking or frustrating because it cannot be accounted for or controlled in a way that allows the subject to feel safe, it registers as a trace. This idea is not outside of psychoanalytic theory, as Ettinger explains that it is Freud himself who leads her here through his idea of the uncanny, or the place that is familiar as if one has been there before (Freud, 1919), which she identifies as the original feminine difference. This uncanny, she argues, is the co-emergence of the I/Not-I of pre-Oedipal subjectivity. For Kristeva, abjection is what causes the infant to react with revulsion toward the uncanny as a means to become a subject, giving in to the aforementioned violence of castration. However, Ettinger offers a way to think about the draw to the uncanny and not just in a way that tantalizes, but which holds us. While the infant may move away from the mother via abjection, she also is always already in contact with her, coming from her womb, made up of her body. Prior to abjection, the mother's body held the infant's body, producing an element of the unconscious that is always premised on the awareness of shared borderspaces and borderlinking. The borderline, then, who disturbs the other moves both into this interstitial space in which beings are substituted for partial objects, in contrast to part-objects, which rely on the bodily orifices and are instead uncentered, like touch. In this sense, she touches the other in a way that language has failed to do via borderlinking, which meaning cannot stand in for.

The implications this has for neoliberal capitalist subjectivity are complex. However, an extension of the unconscious that always indexes another, threatens the neoliberal assumption of individuality, as well as means that the human subject will never quite be able to be an island unto himself. The borderline, like previous feminine monsters, fails to remain within her constellation of signifiers, especially ones that demarcate her as an "I." Psychiatry has been quick to pathologize this, and yet those who specialize in pathology are the ones whom she troubles the most. To reiterate, this is not to say that women with BPD do not suffer, but rather, even in their attempts to "get better," there may always remain a surplus that will not adhere to conventional subjectivity, and will especially not adhere to phallic pronouncements of what a Woman is.

The implications this has on capitalism should be immediately obvious as well. First off, capitalism, in its current manifestation, relies on the celebration of individuality and the cultivation of the self through commodities. If capitalism is relying on the unconscious to market to us as posited by Skott-Myhre (2014), turning our very subjectivity into a commodity, then the borderline, as a liminal space, is pure creative production that relies specifically on rejecting whatever the borders are composed of, whether it be religious doctrine, psychiatric intervention, or capital. The acts of harm against her body scramble the imaginary codes of the body which dictate both what it is and what it means. Rather than enjoying her body and employing an image in the name of the body to which she can relate to, she attacks it, identifying it as a site of capture. This is particularly harmful to the contemporary neoliberal project that celebrates every body as beautiful, colonizing more forms under the patriarchal gaze. If every body is beautiful then every body can also participate in the practices that regulate sexual practices because it has now been deemed desirable, which then contributes to the proliferation of sexual identities in the name of another sexual revolution in which everyone's desire will be perfectly accounted for. From a Lacanian and a Deleuzian perspective, this is ideal for capitalism because it is premised on phallic identities, meaning that their sexuality can be seen and marketed to. As soon as there is a name for their sexual proclivities, more and more discourse can circulate about it, and thus limit the space for creative production and experimentation. The borderline, however, in the exacerbated hysteric's position, continues to refuse, always undermining the hegemonic discourse. The borderline as the sight of sexual difference still has the potential to undermine the empty surplus of capitalism because she draws on what cannot be signified. The borderline reminds us of jouissance beyond the phallus, which, by its definition id impossible to commodify.

References

American Psychiatric Association. 2000. *Diagnostic and statistical manual of mental disorders iv-tr*. Washington: American Psychiatric Association.

American Psychiatric Association. (2013). *Diagnostic and statistical manual of mental disorders* (5th edition). Arlington: American Psychiatric Association.

Butler, J. (2006). Foreword: Bracha's Eurydice. In B. Ettinger (Ed.), *The matrixial borderspace* (VII–XI). Minneapolis, MN: University of Minnesota Press.

Deacon, B.J. (2013). The biomedical model of mental disorder: A critical analysis of its validity, utility and effects on psychotherapy research. *Clinical Psychology Review, 33*, 846–861.

Drob, L.R. (2008). *Borderline personality disorder: A Lacanian perspective*. Saarbrucken, Germany: VDM Verlag Dr. Müller.
Ettinger, B. (2006). *The matrixial borderspace*. Minneapolis, MN: University of Minnesota Press.
Foucault, M. (1973). *The birth of the clinic*. New York: Pantheon Books.
Foucault, M. (2006). *History of madness*. London: Routledge.
Foucault, M. (2008). *Psychiatric power: Lectures at the College de France, 1974–1974*. London: Palgrave MacMillan.
Freud, S. (1919). Das Unheimliche. *Imago, 5*, 229–268.
Gold, N. and Kyratsous, M. (2017). Self and identity in borderline personality disorder: Agency and mental time travel. *Journal of Evaluation in Clinical Practice, 23*(5), 1020–1028.
Hicks, E.D. (1991). *Border writing: The multidimensional text*. Minneapolis, MN: University of Minnesota Press.
Jaffe, S.R., Lansing, S., Producers and Lyne, A., Director. (1987). *Fatal attraction*. USA: Paramount Pictures.
Jimenez, M.A. (1997). Gender and psychiatry: Psychiatric conceptions of mental disorders in women, 1960–1994. *Affilia, 12*(2), 154–175.
Kirsch, I. (2011). *The emperor's new drugs: Exploding the antidepressant myth*. New York: Basic Books.
Kreisman, J.J. and Straus, H. (2014). *I hate you-don't leave me: Understanding the borderline personality*. New York: Brilliance Audio.
Kristeva, J. (1982). *Powers of horror: An essay on abjection*. New York: Columbia University.
Malone, K. (2000). Subjectivity and the address to the other: A Lacanian view of some impasses in theory and psychology. *Theory & Psychology, 10*(1), 79–86.
Malone, K. (2016). Some liminal spaces in Lacanian psychoanalysis. In H. Skott-Myhre, V. Pacini-Ketchabaw and K.S.G. Skott-Myhre (Eds.), *Youth work, early education, and psychology: Liminal encounters* (195–215). New York: Palgrave MacMillan.
Morris, B. (2018). We've always been borderline: Understanding borderline personality disorder as the site of radical subjectivity. *Free Associations, 71*, 51–64.
Pollack, G. (2006). Femininity: Aporia or sexual difference? In B. Ettinger (Ed.), *The matrixial borderspace* (1–40). Minneapolis, MN: University of Minnesota Press.
Sansome, R.A. and Sansome, L.A. (2011). Gender patterns in borderline personality disorder. *Innovations in Clinical Neuroscience, 8*(5), 16–20.
Schwartz-Salant, N. (1987). The dead self in borderline personality disorder. In D.M. Levin (Ed.), *Pathologies of the modern self: Postmodern studies on narcissism, schizophrenia and depression* (84–113). New York: New York University Press.
Skott-Myhre, H. (2014). Schizoanalysis: Seizing desire as the first act of revolutionary psychotherapy. *Psychotherapy and Politics International, 12*(3), 185–195.
Skott-Myhre, H. (2016). Serious play: Youth and the deployment of culturally subversive sign within postmodern capitalism. In J. Wyn and R. White (Eds.), *Handbook of childhood and youth studies* (789–799). New York: Springer.
Skott-Myhre, H., Pacini-Ketchabaw, V. and Skott-Myhre, K.S.G. (2016). *Youth work, early education and psychology: Liminal encounters*. New York: Palgrave Macmillan.

Strong, M. (1998). *A bright red scream: Self-mutilation and the language of pain.* London: Penguin Books.
Sugarman, J. (2015). Neoliberalism and psychological ethics. *Journal of Theoretical and Philosophical Psychology, 35*(2), 103–116.
U'Ren, R. (1997). Psychiatry and capitalism. *The Journal of Mind and Behavior, 18*(1), 1–11.
Wirth-Cauchon, J. (2001). *Women and borderline personality disorder: Symptoms and stories.* New Brunswick, NJ: Rutgers University Press.

Chapter 8

The monster is in the meme

Transgender people and sexual difference

This final chapter attempts to enter into the contemporary conversation about transgender individuals, in particular transwomen, and more specifically, what bathrooms they use. While gaining more representation in the media, and transrights beginning to be taken seriously within both feminism and society in general, transpeople still face a great deal of prejudice and discrimination. For example, *USA Today* remarked that 2018 has seen the highest amount of violence against transgender people in recent history (Pitofsky, 2018). This demonstrates that while visibility and representation of the transcommunity is on the rise, transpeople remain a group that is still met with much ire. This fear or disgust for a group of people cannot simply be chalked up to ignorance or conservative ideals. As I have been attempting to argue, these assertions ignore the visceral reactions these people have to the identified other. I would first like to explore some of the Lacanian theoretical insights on transpeople and transphobia before investigating some of the popular discourse surrounding transpeople, in particular transwomen. Transwomen offer a new instantiation of the monstrous-feminine that opens up the conversation on gender and sexuation that perhaps was inaccessible due to their lack of visibility. However, it is also important to note where some of the LGBQT+ discourse on trans can be explored further for the radical potential of this visibility, which I argue can be redeemed via Deleuze and Guattari's understanding of becoming-woman.

Lacanian perspectives on transgender

With a growing concern regarding the inclusion of gender dysphoria disorder in the *Diagnostic and Statistical Manual of Mental Disorders 5*, psychoanalysts have been quick to contribute to the discussion, offering insights and case studies from their practice. Within the Lacanian tradition, it has been an assumption that a transgender person would likely be psychotically structured, which is now being criticized and reconsidered to not only consider the social conditions, but also to remain faithful to the practice by not asserting a diagnosis hastily or haphazardly. However, there is a growing interest in how to understand the gender transformation as a symptom, while also not contributing to further stigmatization of the community. Analysts Genèvieve Morel and Patricia Gherovici have articulated the most comprehensive views on the transgender person in the clinic, or transsexuality as it is commonly referred to within Lacanian theory. It should be noted that while in popular discourse, "transsexual" is falling out of favor, it is still used within Lacanian psychoanalysis in order to refer to the sexed subject, as there is no gendered subject of the unconscious. Gender refers to the stylized presentation of one's ego, whereas the sexed subject is the subject referred to in sexuation—as having or being the phallus. Both Morel and Gherovici return to Lacan's patients that have been designated as trannsexuals, as well as their own case studies, to take up the psychosis versus sinthome debate.

In 1990, Catherine Millot claimed that transsexuals likely occupied a psychotic position, an assertion she made based on a prevalent fantasy of a sex that was not lacking and therefore outside of sexuation or sexual difference. This idea has been more or less supported among the Lacanian community for some time. Lattanzio and Carvalho Ribeiro (2017) provide an excellent summary of this perspective, which they outline as being one of four propositions: 1) that the person is convinced of being a woman imprisoned in a man's body as a baseline for psychosis; 2) the penis is confused for the phallus and thus a foreclosure on the Name of the Father; 3) such a condition emerges from or is enhanced by the discourses of science and capitalism; and 4) within transsexuality, the imaginary achieves the same pertinence as in other psychoses (p. 73). Similarly, Geldof and Verhaeghe (2017) suggest that increasing trend in identifying as "queer" is an attempt to deny castration. Morel (2000) explains this as what she calls a "common error" (p. 184). This common error, according to Morel, is when the phallus has been foreclosed upon as a result of the refusal to correlate the phallus to jouissance. Instead, the subject must concoct a way of "anchoring jouissance" (p. 184). For Morel, this is the reason that the transsubject is psychotically structured, as evidenced in her case studies she provides.

It is not my prerogative to debate whether or not the transsubjects Morel was working with were psychotically structured, or even to debate the claim that transpeople are likely to be psychotically structured or not. Rather, I am interested in the discourse around the use of the term "psychotic," with some analysts, like Morel, Millot, and Verhaeghe, remaining more traditional in their interpretations, whereas Gherovici and Cavanagh consider the way the word "psychotic" comes with further stigma. Gherovici (2019) rightfully argues that the tendency to provide a blanket diagnosis of psychosis to transpeople stems from the assumption that Freud's patient's, Judge Schreber, psychosis, and trannsexualism were mutually exclusive. She advocates instead for a differential clinic that would preserve the subjectivity of the patient. Gherovici's demonstrates this by asserting that there is a difference between a transsexual delusion and transsexuality resulting in a gender reassignment surgery. As Cavanagh (2016) explains, Gheorvici uses Lacan's patient, Primeau, to demonstrate that though he expressed a concern he was turning into a woman, he was not necessarily looking to affirm that he was in fact a woman. Rather, he had a trannsexual delusion, meaning that one could be psychotic with a trannsexual symptom, but that the logical assumption is not then that all transpeople are psychotic. In fact, Gherovici demonstrates that Lacan was careful not to assume this and refrained from taking any sort of definitive stance toward gender assignment surgery.

Both Gherovici and Cavanagh suggest understanding trannsexuality as a sinthome, meaning that it is not a symptom predicated on an address to the Other, but rather a means through which to regulate jouissance. As Lacan (2016) explains, the experience of anxiety should be understood as a lack of a lack, meaning that there is no room for the subject in the unconscious. As Cavanagh explains, the memoirs and art pieces by transpeople tend to demonstrate a painful excess that cannot be contained by the body that results in a feeling of self-enclosure. Gherovici (2019) suggests that transitioning may be an attempt to reclaim the body and reinstate lack. Similarly, queer theorist Sheila Cavanagh (2016), relying on Bracha Ettingers's theory of the matrixial substratum of subjectivity discussed in an earlier chapter, suggests that transsexuality can be understood as a sinthome through which to creatively engage with Other jouissance that has been foreclosed upon in the phallic stratum. Such an approach does not simply aim to remove the stigma associated with psychosis, but to understand transsexuality as a generative artistic expression of the unconscious.

While most within the debate are analysts and tend to return to the assumed neutrality of the clinic, though usually indexing the history of controversial relationship between people in the LGBQT+ community and psychoanalysis, there seems to be a tension as to how to appropriately deal with the transperson. This attempt to understand or know what the transperson does, as Gherovic suggests, we do not do, which is to compromise the subjectivity of the individual, making trans an encompassing group about which one can know something. Psychoanalysis gets caught in a bind in which it can offer something, perhaps even something liberatory, to a sensitive group of people who are frequently the victims of violence and discrimination, while also contributing to the reification of their status as such. Psychoanalysis, however, also has the unique opportunity to discuss otherness and difference in an insightful way. In turning next to some of the discourses about transpeople in the popular culture, it is my intention to do so with the belief that these are a group of people who sit at the locus of an important political discussion, and not my intention to make light of the violent rhetoric and actions directed at them.

The monster in the next stall

At the center of the transgender discourse in the United States has been the question of what bathroom transgender people should use. This question has been at the center of legal trials and political campaigns, with President Obama issuing a directive to schools to allow transgender students to use the bathroom of their choice, followed by President Trump quickly rescinding it (Hawkins, 2017). During his presidential campaign in 2016, Senator Ted Cruz advocated harshly against the transgender inclusive policy, claiming that the country has gone "stark raving nuts" (Gabriel, 2016). Three years later, both North Carolina and Virginia are back in the courts over the issue with groups on both sides citing an infringement on their rights to safety and privacy.

Rather than restaging or evaluating the debate, my interest here is the discourse used by those against the transgender bathroom policies and the ways in which that has been taken up in popular discourse, especially through the use of memes. Swales (2018) provides and considered and apt explanation of a Lacanian interpretation of this specific debate. She suggests that the appearance of a transgender person in a bathroom in particular disrupts the fantasy of the sexed binary in which the body is interpreted as the locus of gender. She further this, following Lacan (1998), by suggesting that the bathroom is already a place in which bodies are unstable and susceptible to fragmentation due to the natural bodily functions that occur in this space. Transphobia, then, is the attempt to defend against this intrusion and to reify the fantasy of the contained body, as well as the body as binarily sexed according to gender.

This issue has not been contained to the realm of politics and legal trials, however, and many anti-transrhetoric can be found in all corners of the internet. One particularly popular method for disseminating information, especially information that relies on an affectual trigger, is through memes. Richard Dawkins originally coined the term "meme" to refer to an idea that organically reproduces and spreads throughout society (Cooper, 2018). Internet memes have become a new language, especially among the millennial and younger generations. They typically pair an ambiguous image, such as a cartoon penguin, with a quick statement reflecting a perspective on a situation, person, or social issue. For example, socially awkward penguin is simply a cartoon character that people attach statements that reflect social anxiety such as, "Someone bumps into you, apologize." Ross and Rivers (2017) explain how memes have provided an opportunity for several demographics to participate in political discourse, as well as how memes are used to delegitimize discourse. They argue that this occurs by questioning the legitimacy of the authority of the person in question, a moral evaluation that is sometimes quite subtle, rationalization or appeals to "the way things are," and through the use of cautionary tales. In regard to the experiences of transpeople, it can easily be argued that antitransmemes seek to delegitimize the concerns of the community and its allies, resulting in a flattening of the political discourse.

From a psychoanalytic perspective, however, these memes tend to reveal deeper concerns. First off, a quick google search for "antitransmemes" tends to produce hundreds of images of transwomen, and very few transmen. If memes can be read as a symptom, the anxiety about transmen in the same bathroom as cismen does not seem to be as much of a concern for the antitransgroup as transwomen in the women's bathroom. At first glance it may seem to reflect a concern about male desire, evoking the often-cited evolutionary assumption that male sexual desire is both more virile and unruly than women's. This is reflected in the "common sense" arguments in the bathroom debate as well. As Ron Baity, president of Return America and a pastor in North Carolina, states, "He could be there to look at the anatomy of the opposite sex. He could be there because he's a sex pervert. He could be there to bring damage to a young girl" (Brady, 2016). As Brady points out it in this article, the anecdotal evidence typically used to support these points comes from crime reports of men using women's clothing to sneak into women's bathrooms, and not actual transindividuals. Similarly, many memes depict men with badly applied makeup, and haphazardly dressed, sometimes with their genitalia exposed, accompanied with text with something to the effect that this is who wants in the restroom with your daughter/wife, though the daughter seems to be the preferred threat. One meme is a split picture, with a man emerging from a bathroom stall in the ladies room in a full business suit, with the words "I became a woman 2 minutes ago" and the second picture depicting a blue male bathroom symbol peaking over a wall at the red female bathroom symbol with the words "coming soon to a restroom near you." The pictures are supposed to be excessive and emphasize a concern about the predatory nature of men, whereas memes generated by the actual transcommunity reflect the opposite. They tend to reflect transpeople who appear less ambiguously, that is they look like their gender, in contrast to the antitransmemes, which sometimes depict a man with a strewn wig or smeared makeup. Transfriendly memes also demonstrate how out of place they appear in the wrong bathroom. Interestingly enough, the pro-transmemes tend to also emphasize transmen in women's bathroom, speaking to the public's concern of a man in a woman's place, though the perhaps more prescient concern would be a transwoman in a man's bathroom.

Regardless, the conflation with sexual predators and transwomen in both the discourse of politicians and community leaders, as well as memes, tend to rely on the primacy of the phallus as signification. In both the cases of cisgender men and transwomen, there is a greater chance that the penis is present, though there are of course transwomen and transmen who have had gender affirming surgery. In fact, many of the memes and opinion pieces I encountered emphasized the presence of biological markers for maleness.

For example, one meme, featuring a transgender woman in business attire, claims that "no one cares that you're transgender/we care that you have a penis and think it is ok to compete professionally against women." What is interesting about this meme is that it names the problem—the penis—rather than alluding to it, like in the other memes. However, while the other memes suggest a potential sexual assault, whereby the penis would be involved, this one refers to the penis when it would unlikely to be involved in most occupational competitions. This meme in particular demonstrates the mistaken assumption that the penis is the phallus and therefore, as long as it is present, the source of enjoyment that comes with it must also be, regardless if that is sexual pleasure, or the phallic jouissance of occupational success. This is also reflected in the number of controversies surrounding transgender athletes, in particular transwomen competing against ciswomen. Currently, there is a civil rights probe occurring in Connecticut for their policy on allowing transwomen to compete as the gender that they identify, with many critics suggesting that the higher levels of testosterone and muscle mass in transwomen gives them an unfair advantage against ciswomen (Associated Press, 2019). This is not to say that this cannot be the case, but that much of the conversations and controversy reflect a concern about the state of phallic enjoyment.

The "horror" surrounding transgender inclusivity seems to be directed almost entirely at transwomen. Again, I refer specifically to transwomen, because though transmen are the victims of violence and discrimination, there does not seem to be the same amount of public discourse produced about them, which from a Lacanian perspective means that there is less anxiety about them. This could be in part that it has long been more acceptable for women to dabble with male attire and affect without compromising her identity, sexuality, or sexual orientation. If I wear pants and a blazer one day following a dress, my students do not question my sexuality or mental health, though this would unfortunately be less likely if my male colleagues showed up to class in makeup or a dress. This, however, does not mean that transmen are more accepted in our society, as it is still likened to a "dressing up." Transgender men face numerous challenges including custody issues, privacy issues, and are referred to by several derogatory names. I am not trying to suggest that this is not the case. However, when it comes to the bathroom debate, there seems to be less memes generated about them, with memes being emblematic of the basest level of cultural discourse. What I am attempting to contend is that if the bathroom debate was really about the safety and security of those with vaginas from those with penises, the real issue would be transmen in men's bathrooms, as it would be possible that transmen would still have vaginas and would be surrounded by multiple people with penises. And yet, this is less likely represented. In fact, when it is represented, it is usually from the transcommunity, emphasizing the danger of asking them to use bathrooms that do not correspond to their gender identity.

Perhaps one of the reasons that transwomen are positioned as monstrous could be said to reflect an anxiety about the misunderstanding and the conflation between the penis and the phallus. The lack of discourse around transmen actually further emphasizes the importance of the fantasy of the phallus. Transmen could be said to participate in the illusion that men have the phallus by adopting masculine qualities that correspond to an identity premised in having rather than being the phallus. To challenge a transman's lack of phallus means having to contend with one's own lack of phallus. Perhaps this is why when this does occur, such as in the film *Boys Don't Cry*, a sexual assault also occurs, whereby a man or men must violently demonstrate that they are the true bearers of the phallus, and since they are unable to do this, they must expose the lack in the other in order to veil their own.

It is important to note that, from a Lacanian perspective, much of the popular discourse around transgenderism misses out on some of the truly radical political potential of Lacan's understanding of sexuation. Contemporary transgender discourse relies on a refurbished gender essentialism, in which one's body does not correspond to one's internal gender. Appeals to neuroscience and psychology seek to confirm such assertions. While scholars and activists dedicated to transgender politics have the opportunity to challenge the gender binary and gender essentialism, these appeals to a gendered brain or psychology inadvertently accept certain problematic assumptions, such as that gender performativity is a biological expression of one's true nature. Furthermore, in Lacanian terms, assuming a gender identity will always rely on the assertion of having signification that corresponds to that gender, whether it is a dress or a beard, and therefore, is always on the masculine side of sexuation. The current proliferation of gender identities inevitably reifies the phallicization of sexed identity rather than react against patriarchal norms.

This is not to say that the representation of gender identities has not been important for increasing awareness and acceptance of diverse expressions of gender and sexuality. However, it is important to consider the ever-expanding representations of sexual expression under the context of neoliberal capitalism and ask, if it is being sold to us, does it have its political potential any longer? Furthermore, are demands for representation demands to be further inscribed and accounted for within capitalism, and therefore void of political validity? I believe that this argument is a fair one and reflects concern about capitalism's ability to appropriate politically viable alternatives to its own ideologies. While I am sympathetic to this argument, I have been attempting to demonstrate that the prevalence of anxiety in reaction to aberrant individuals across many different sociohistorical contexts indicates an almost ungovernable excess between the assumed norm and the identified other. The representation of transgender people may itself not be the political gesture to undermine capitalist ideology, but as those distinctly other, their public presence may allow for the disturbance of concretized identities and afford the opportunity to discuss Deleuze's becoming-woman in the 21st century.

Becoming-trans

Many scholars have written extensively about transgenderism being foundationally important in theories pertaining to gender and sexuality, so I will not reiterate that here. Rather, I would like to return to where I began this book, with an interest in allowing a disjunctive synthesis between Lacan and Deleuze to produce creative ways of thinking about those people on the fringes of society. We are at a particularly interesting moment in time regarding conversations about gender and sexuality, with more and more people being represented as within the norm of gender expression. Though it may be fair to claim that a change in gender norms does not correspond to a change in sexuation or even neurotic structure, exploring the potential latent in this recent manifestation of identities may provide an opportunity to return to the question of subjectivity in contemporary politics and social action.

Nikki Sullivan (2006) investigates this question by turning to bodily modification practices in general and emphasizing those surgeries that aim to align with a different gender as being a response to an Other within. She situates body modification practices as "trans" practices, suggesting that the surgeries undertaken by transgendered individuals can be understood within a larger arena of cultural practices for their commitment to transform the bodily being. In doing so, the body becomes understood as the site of inscription processes, rather than a static object, and which practices are deemed socially acceptable and which are morally condemned become subject to a critical social evaluation. In doing so, Sullivan is interested in those practices that specifically distort, exaggerate, or challenge the natural state of the body that may produce feelings of shock, disgust, or even horror from the spectator, practices which she refers to as "transmogrification." She understands this transmogrification as an attempt to navigate the boundary between self and other and attempts to offer what she refers to as an "intercorporeal ethics" as a means for relating to those relegated to the abject or monstrous in exchange for the ongoing moral condemnation those identified others face. This approach challenges assumed notions of transsexualism and deviates from the analytic clinic by taking a more postmodern approach to the body. Sullivan, following Califia (1997) and Nataf (1996), argues that transgenderism exploits the already ambiguous and fluid nature of the body.

Sullivan's approach seems to embrace Braidotti's (2002, 2013) neo-materialist framework for the posthuman. For Braidotti, the posthuman relies on an immanentest understanding of the human, in which the mind and body are one, and assumes matter to be intelligent and self-organizing. This follows the Spinozist tradition, which claims we do not know yet what the body can do. The body is relationally embedded and affected and thus co-extensive with the living force of the social body, meaning not only the discourses and ideologies, but also the excluded excesses. This has radical implications when considering transgenderism. As Sullivan articulates, body modification already demonstrates the ways in which the body is in flux with the socius, expanding the limits of the assumed knowledge of what a body is and what it can do. Transgenderism take this a step further, demonstrating the ways in which ideology and discourses are inscribed on the lived body, but also that the lived body responds and morphs, blunting the sharp chisel of normative discourses that attempt to render the body inert. With the ongoing bathroom discourses, we are seeing the body confront structures and institutions, forcing them to rearrange themselves. Sometimes this is as simple as replacing a sticker on a door, and sometimes this is more creative, such as in the case of Esther Sperber's suggestion to provide bathrooms that correspond to size needs, so that urinals are a small bathroom, people with children or luggage use large bathrooms, etc. (Wong, 2016).

From a Lacanian perspective, the body is always already trans. What I mean by this is that the body is always constituted by another. The subject must rely on another to tell him or her what his or her body signifies. Just as psychosomatic symptoms that inscribe themselves on the body as an address to an Other, the body itself is only understood through the Other's addresses. This is the foundation of Lacan's mirror stage, in which the subject must be spoken into being. However, this being, or ego, for Lacan, is always a misrecognition. In order for there to be a concrete "I," I need to believe there is a concrete "You," but "I" and "You" only occur in relation and through identification. This identification relies on assumptions that are inaccurate—who has the phallus and who does not. When the transgender body challenges the significations of the body, whether it be "male," "female," "you," or "I," it opens up a line of flight. Fournier (2014) demonstrates that Massumi's (1987) translation of "ligne de fuite," where "fuite" means the act of fleeing or eluding, also means flowing or leaking. He goes on to say that feeling as if one is not the correct gender is also a moment of such leaking, whereby there are cracks in the "I" or who you believe yourself to be. It is because of their ability to evoke a noticeable affect about the assumed static gender categories that transpeople and gender nonconforming people are able to potentially produce cracks in those rigid, phallic symbols.

As I have suggested earlier, this sort of encounter with a transperson has the potential to cause anxiety about what one does not have, resulting in discrimination and violence against the transgender person. However, there is also potential in such an encounter to produce a new expression of affect of and between bodies, that is, to effect a becoming. As Sullivan points out becoming emphasizes difference for difference sake, demonstrating that there is no one, or in this case two, bodies to which all other bodies correspond to. Just as Deleuze and Guattari (year) call for the monstrous babies of philosophy, there is a question if the body or subject that offends and deemed monstrous is actually a site of creativity, both for the individual and those which she encounters. Shildrick argues that the monster, or the abjected, is the site of what Merleu-Ponty refers to as the chiasm, which rejects the dualism of self and other, and forces an encounter with the other in the self. This is perhaps the best point at which to once more return to Lacanian theory. An encounter with another that elicits anxiety does so because it is also an encounter with our notion of a primal Other, who places demands upon us, yet can never be satisfied. When an encounter can undermine the assumed integrity of the body, such as the case of an encounter with a transgender person, there is potential for a brief moment of compassion, not just in the sense of concern, but to suffer with. In such encounters, what is important is not the two individuals that enter into a conversation, dance, or fight, but rather what emerges through them.

The question ultimately comes to: how do we as activists and those interested in radical politics both understand these encounters between the monstrous and the hegemonic, while also respecting and caring for those on the fringes. It is quite often the case that those on the fringes, though we may identify ways in which they are undermining the status quo, desperately want to be matriculated into the same society that they stand in opposition to. If capitalism appropriates everything, should we be suspicious of what becomes accepted and commonplace in society, or should we celebrate when inclusivity is respected? Perhaps this is where Braidotti's notion of nomadic subjectivity is helpful. Braidotti understands that it is essential that we challenge phallic signification such as "man" or "woman" but that to do away with those significations can be harmful. She advocates for experimenting with signification, and clinging to it when in hostile territory, but knowing when to relinquish those signifiers of identity when one can. What is important is determining who is assigning the signification and why. For example, as Fournier points out, "The product of particular intensities—your body processing hormones, clothing, surgery, moods, environment—becomes a pattern of signs, read through social patterns re/territorializing transgender bodies" (p. 122). However, perhaps what we are witnessing in the contemporary moment is the expansion of the signifiers "man" and "woman," which may have the potential to also augment the sexual nonrapport in a way that asks for a creative response to the question of the other's desire, and hopefully disrupting the habitual phobic responses.

***

I have attempted to provide a means of thinking about the classification of certain types of women as monstrous, which does not simply reduce this designation to mere misogyny or patriarchal practices. Though the identification of discriminatory practices is useful, they do not speak to the underlying motives, which are not inconsequential. It is also not satisfactory to take a cognitive-behavioral approach to such practices, assuming that once a behavior is deemed misogynistic or discriminatory or the conscious motivations are determined, it will cease. The behaviors, and the thoughts and emotions associated with them seem to become more insidious instead. Instead, the unconscious as something produced between subjects needs to be taken seriously for the ways it attempts to answer questions about the otherness of the other. While there are several groups of people who have been relegated to the position of "other," Lacan's understanding of sexuation provides a means through which to consider a relation to a primal Other. For those concerned about the role of subjectivity in socio-political discourse, an understanding of sexuation allows for a way to consider those subjects who seem to possess the latent potential to disturb phallic subjectivity, and produce creative encounters. These encounters, of course, have not been the answer to ridding us of that phallic or molarized subjectivity, but rather, "monsters" present the socius with a demand that could not be accounted for. It is these subjects which provoke a reorganization of significations which attempt to, and fail to, account for the Woman.

References

Associated Press. (2019, August 9). Civil rights probe opened into transgender athlete policy. *NBC News*. Retrieved from www.nbcnews.com/feature/nbc-out/civil-rights-probeopened-transgender-athlete-policy-n1040796

Brady, J. (2016, May 15). When a transgender person uses a public bathroom, who is at risk? *NPR*. Retrieved from www.npr.org/2016/05/15/477954537/when-a-transgenderperson-uses-a-public-bathroom-who-is-at-risk

Braidotti, R. (2002). *Metapmorphoses: Towards a feminist becoming*. Cambridge: Polity.

Braidotti, R. (2013). *The posthuman*. Cambridge: Polity.

Califia, P. (1997). *Sex changes: The politics of transgender*. Minneapolis, MN: Cleis Press.

Cavanagh, S.L. (2016). Transsexuality as sinthome: Bracha L. Ettinger and the other (feminine) sexual difference. *Studies in Gender and Sexuality*, *17*(1), 27–44.

Cooper, P.G. (2018). Internet memes. *Salem Press Encyclopedia*. Retrieved from http://search.ebscohost.com.proxy.library.brocku.ca/login.aspx?direct=true&db=ers&A=89138977&site=eds-live&scope=site

Fournier, M. (2014). Lines of flight. *Transgender Studies Quarterly*, *1*(1–2), 121–122.

Gabriel, T. (2016, April 29). Ted Cruz, attacking Donald Trump, uses transgender bathroom access as cudgel. *The New York Times*. Retrieved from www.nytimes.com/2016/04/30/us/politics/indiana-republican-transgender-rightsbathroom.html

Geldof, A. and Verhaghe, P. (2017). Queer as a new shelter from castration. In N. Giffney and E. Watson (Eds.), *Clinical encounters in sexuality: Psychoanalytic practice and queer theory* (211–221). Santa Barbara, CA: Punctum Books.

Gherovici, P. (2019). Transgender expressions and psychosis: Towards and ethics of sexual difference. *British Journal of Psychotherapy*, *35*(3), 417–430.

Hawkins, D. (2017, February 23). The short, troubled life of Obama's transgender student protections. *The Washington Post*. Retrieved from www.washingtonpost.com/news/morning-mix/wp/2017/02/23/the-short-troubledlife-of-obamas-transgender-student-protections/?noredirect=on

Lacan, J. (1998). *The four fundamental concepts of psychoanalysis: Book XI.* New York: W.W. Norton & Co.
Lacan, J. (2016). *Anxiety: Book X.* Cambridge: Polity.
Lattanzio, F.F. and Carvalho Ribeiro, P. (2017). Transsexuality, psychosis and originary femininity: Between psychoanalysis and feminist theory. *Psicologia USP, 28*(1), 72–82.
Massumi, B. (1987). Notes on the translation and acknowledgements. In G. Deleuze and F. Guattari (Eds.), *A thousand plateaus* (xvii–xx). Minneapolis, MN: University of Minnesota Press.
Millot, C. (1990). *Horsexe: Essay on transsexuality.* New York: Autonomedia.
Morel, G. (2000). *Sexual ambiguities.* London: Routledge.
Nataf, Z. (1996). *Lesbians talk transgender.* London: Scarlet Press.
Pitofsky, M. (2018, September 18). "Epidemic of violence": 2018 is the worst for deadly assaults against transgender Americans. *USA Today.* Retrieved from www.usatoday.com/story/news/2018/09/26/2018-deadliest-year-transgenderdeathsviolence/1378001002/
Ross, A.S. and Rivers, D.J. (2017). Digital cultures of political participation: Internet memes and the discursive delegitimization of the 2016 US presidential candidates. *Discourse, Context & Media, 16,* 1–11.
Sullivan, N. (2006). Transmogrification: (Un)becoming other(s). In S. Stryker and S. Whittle (Eds.), *The transgender studies reader.* New York: Routledge.
Swales, S. (2018). Transphobia in the bathroom: Sexual difference, alterity and jouissance. *Psychoanalysis, Culture and Society, 23*(3), 290–309.
Wong, C.M. (2016, July 13). Here's a creative solution to the transgender "bathroom bill" war. *Huffington Post.* Retrieved from www.huffpost.com/entry/transgender-bathroomesther-sperber_n_5783e590e4b01edea78ef6da

Index

abject theory 3, 5; borderline subjectivity and 115–8; Christianity identification of 37; in film and fantasy 57; Kristeva and 2, 22–4, 46; in mythology 46–8; and neoliberal capitalism 113–4
Adam 36
Aguilera, C. 97
Alien (film) 59
American feminism, concerns of 1
American Psychiatric Association 112
Anthony, C. 77
Antichrist (film) 73, 75–6
Anti-Oedipus: Capitalism and schizophrenia (Deleuze and Guattari) 24, 25, 84
Apple, F. 97, 98
Aronofsky, D. 76
Aronson, A. 73
Aster, A. 73–4

Baartman, S. 1
Babadook, The (film) 73, 76
Babylonian Talmud 36–7
bad breast 79
Baity, R. 128
Basic Instinct (film) 99, 100–2, 107–8
bathrooms, transgender people and 127–31
Beckman, F. 99
becoming-woman theory 2–3, 7. *See also* sexuation; becoming multiple and 60–3; Deleuze and Guattari on 24–9; mythology and encounters with 45–8; sexuation and 10–29
Beyond the pleasure principle (Freud) 33
Bible, women in 36–9
birth of the clinic, The (Foucault) 50–1
blue pilled 105
Bodies without Organs (BwO) 61, 62

body modification practices 131–2
borderline personality disorder (BPD) 111–21; abjection and 115–8; borderline subject described 111; described 112–3; gender neutrality and 112–3; liminal spaces, borderlinking and 119–21; neoliberal capitalism and 113–5; women with 120–1
borderline subject: abjection and 115–8; described 111; identity disturbance and 117–8; neoliberal capitalism and 111, 113–5; self-harming behavior and 116–7; term uses for 112–3
borderlinking, liminal spaces and 119–21
Boys Don't Cry (film) 130
BPD. *See* borderline personality disorder (BPD)
Braidotti, R. 28–9, 60, 61, 83, 106, 131, 133
Break of Noon (play) 103–4
British Gazeteer, The 54
British Medical Journal, The 53–4, 59
Broedel, H. P. 43
Brood, The (film) 57, 59
Butler, J. 20, 68, 119

Califia, P. 131
Canguilhem, G. 61
Carter, A. 94–5
Carvalho Ribeiro, P. 125
castration anxiety 4–5, 16, 18, 24, 29, 33–5, 38–9, 56, 59, 66–7, 72, 101–2, 125
Cavanagh, S. L. 86, 126
Chamber of Bloody Secrets, The (Carter) 94
Cixous, H. 68
Claudel, P. 103

Clover, C. 3–4, 6, 73
Colebrook, C. 47
Collette, T. 74
common error 125
Copjec, J. 12, 17
Cowlie, E. 99–100
Creed, B. 3, 4–6, 33, 34, 57, 73
Cronenberg, D. 57, 59
Cruz, T. 127

Dafoe, W. 75
Dawkins, R. 127
death, jouissance and 105–8
de Beauvoir, S. 60
Deleuze, G. 2–3, 7, 24–6, 62, 106; on becoming-woman 26–9; Bodies without Organs (BwO) and 61; liminal spaces and 119; molar identity of woman and 26, 47, 82; mouth-breast assemblage and 106
del Rey, L. 97
Diagnosis and Statistical Manual of Mental Disorders (DSM) 5, 112, 124
Dietz, P. 78
Doane, M. A. 99
Douglas, M. 23–4

"Ecstasy of St. Teresa, The" (Bernini statue) 39–40
Ego Psychology 11
Ettinger, B. 21, 68, 85–6, 119–20, 126
Evanescence 97
Eve 36, 37
Exorcist, The (film) 59

Fatal Attraction (film) 102, 107–8, 113
Felman, S. 20–1, 66
feminine jouissance 15, 17, 19–20; becoming-woman and 45–8; saints and 39–42; witches and 42–5
femme fatales, fairytales and 89–108; characteristics of 90–1; Evil Queen, Snow White and 91–6; jouissance, death and 105–8; melancholic feminine 89–90; and men who hate them 104–5; MGTOW's and 104–5; overview of 89; pop music, melancholic feminine of 96–9; woman who has it all 99–104
films: final girl 3–4; masculine fantasy 100–3; maternal grief 73; monster in 72–6; used in study of horror 6–9; used in study of sexual difference 6–9
final girl films 3–4
Fink, B. 11, 14–5, 20, 69, 70, 71, 81
Foucault, M. 50–1, 114. *See also* medical gaze, sexual difference and
Fournier, M. 132
Freidan, B. 77
French feminism, concerns of 1
Freud, S. 24, 33, 38, 65, 120; Little Hans case 67; Madonna-Whore complex 79; on sexuality 66–7
Friday the 13th (film) 91

Gainsbourg, C. 75
Geldof, A. 125
gender theory 3
gender *vs.* sexed subject 125
Genre (Neale) 5
George, S. 21, 60
Gherovici, P. 70, 125–6
Girl with the Dragon Tattoo, The (film) 107
Gone Girl (film) 99, 101, 102
good breast 79
Gossip Girl (TV show) 107
Grande, A. 98
Greek mythology. *See* mythology, sexual difference in
Greek sphinx, as monstrous-feminine 35
Grosz, E. 20, 22, 23
Grudge, The (film) 72
Guattari, F. 2–3, 7, 24–6; on becoming-woman 26–9; Bodies without Organs (BwO) and 61; liminal spaces and 119; molar identity of woman and 26, 47, 82; mouth-breast assemblage and 106

Hadewijch 39
Harvey, K. 54, 55
#MeToo 1
heartbeat bill 56
Hereditary (film) 59, 73–5
Hicks, E. D. 116
Hollandsworth, S. 77
Homer 34
Hook, D. 21, 60
horror: described 2; film use in study of 6–9; final girl films and 3–4; sexual difference and 2, 3–6

House of psychotic women (Janisse) 5
human dissection 41

identity disturbance 117–8
Imaginary: described 12; Lacanian psychoanalysis and 12–3
in-between subject 111
Inception (film) 99
Institoris, H. 44–5
Irigaray, L. 20, 22, 68
It Follows (film) 72–3

Jancovich, M. 91
Janisse, K. L. 5
Jewel 97
Johnson, S. 89
Joplin, J. 96
jouissance 20; death and 105–8; feminine 15, 17, 19–20; Lacanian psychoanalysis and 14–5; of Other relationship 14–5; Other's, depicted in *It Follows* 72–3; saints and feminine 39–42; sexuation and 14–5; witches and feminine 42–5
Joyce, J. 27

Kaplan, E. A. 103
Kellermann, N. P. 56
Kempe, M. 40
Kent, J. 76
Kernberg, O. 117
Kill Bill (film) 107
King, R.D. 25
Klein, M. 10, 79
Kristeva, J. 2, 3, 5, 7, 21, 68, 76, 79, 89–90, 97; abjection and 22–4, 46, 117; Bible, abject and 37; symbolic and 23

Lacan, J. 1, 2, 10, 15, 55, 68, 95, 98, 103. *See also* Lacanian psychoanalysis; on borderline subjective structure 112–3; experience of anxiety and 126; feminine jouissance and 19–20; Freud and 10–1; mirror stage 11, 12; on neurotic structures 69–70; saints and 39–42; sexuation/sexual difference notion of 1–2, 7, 65–6; Woman notion of 3, 16–7, 19
Lacanian psychoanalysis: criticisms of 20–1, 68; described 10–1; Imaginary and 12–3; jouissance and 14–5;

Kristeva and abject theory 22–4; mother-monster 67–70; object a 15; Other relationship and 11, 70–1; perversion and 71–2; politics and 21–9; Real and 12, 13–4, 120; sexual difference and 1–2; sexuation and 15–20; subjects 11–2; Symbolic and 12–3; transgender perspectives of 124–6
Laplanche, J. 58
Laqueur, T. 51–2
Lattanzio, F. F. 125
Lee, A. 97
Levy-Stokes, C. 14
Lilith 36–8
liminal spaces, borderlinking and 119–21
Lurie, S. 5

Madonna-Whore complex 79, 93
male gaze 4
Malleus Maleficarum 43
Malone, K. 119
Mark, Z. M. 15
Marrati, P. 47
masculine fantasy films 100–3
Massumi, B. 25, 84–5, 107, 132
maternal grief films 73
maternal imagination/impressions 52–4
matrixial borderspace theory 119–20, 126
Mazzoni, C. 52, 53
McGowan, T. 21, 105
medical gaze, sexual difference and 50–63; becoming-woman, becoming multiple and 60–3; films and fantasies 57–60; Foucault and 50–1; maternal imagination/impressions and 52–4; monstrous womb fears and 56; overview of 50; Toft story 54–5; trauma and 58
Medusa, as monstrous-feminine 33
melancholic feminine 89–90
memes of transgender people 127–9
Men, women and chain saws: Gender in the modern horror film (Clover) 3–4
"Men Going Their Own Way" (MGTOW) 104–5
Meyers, C. L. 79
MGTOW ("Men Going Their Own Way") 104–5
Mieli, P. 98
Miller, J. A. 103

Millot, C. 125
mirror stage 11, 12
Misery (film) 91
Mitchell, J. 20
molar assemblages 25
molecular assemblages 25; monstrous offspring and 61–3
monstrous-feminine: Greek sphinx as 35; Medusa as 33; in mythology 32–5; Sirens as 33–4; theory 4–6
monstrous-feminine: Film, feminism and psychoanalysis, The (Creed) 3, 4–6
monstrous womb fears 56; molecular (un)consciousnessness and 61–3
Morel, G. 125
Mother! (film) 76
m(O)ther: navigating 72; as nexus 84–6
mother-monster, psychoanalysis and 65–86; in film 72–6; m(O)ther as nexus 84–6; murderous mothers 77–80; obsessive neurotics 81–2; overview of 65–6; unconscious and 67–72; woman in psychoanalysis 66–72; woman-mother, deterritorializing 82–4
mother-monsters in film 72–6; depicting Other's jouissance 72–3; effects of 76; He and She example 75–6; maternal grief themes of 73; that evoke/engage the law 73–5
Mujica, B. 40
Mulvey, L. 4, 6
murderous mothers 77–80; overview of 77; Smith, Susan case 78, 79–80; Yates, Andrea case 78–80
mythology, sexual difference in 32–48; becoming-woman, encounters with 45–8; feminine jouissance, saints and 39–42; feminine jouissance, witches and 42–5; monstrous-feminine in myth 32–5; overview of 32; saints and witches 39–45; women in Bible 36–9

Nancy Grace (TV show) 77
Nataf, Z. 131
National Institute of Mental Health 112
Neale, S. 5
Nedoh, B. 29
neoliberal capitalism, psychiatry and 113–5
neurotic structures 69–70
N'sync 97

Oberman, M. 79
object a 15
obsessive neurotics 81–2
O'Conor, T. 46
Odyssey (Homer) 34
Oedipus Rex 35
Oliver, K. 24
Once Upon a Time (TV series) 92, 93–4
Ordinary Psychoses 73
Other relationship 70; femme fatale and 105–8; *It Follows* depiction of 72–3; jouissance of 14–5; Lacanian psychoanalysis and 11, 70–1; paternal law and 57–9; sexual difference and 1–2; Woman as Other 58–9

Park, K. 41
Parker, I. 21
penis, transgender people and 128–9
perversion 71–2
petite object a 15
phallic/phallus: becoming-woman and 27–9, 45–8, 60–1; criticisms of, in Lacanian theory 20–1; Ettinger's matrixial borderspace theory and 119–20; femme fatale and 93–4, 98–9, 101–2, 108; in films and fantasies 57–8, 72–3; Freudian castration anxiety and 4–5, 66–7, 101; Greek mythology examples of 33–5; jouissance 39–42, 93, 106–7; Kristeva and, law 22–3, 79–80; Lacanian sexuation and 15–20, 68–70; Lacan's jouissance and 14–5, 90; memes 125–6, 128–30; m(O)ther and 72; Neale male monster and 5; Other and inherited signifiers as 13; saints and, jouissance 39–42; Symbolic signifiers and 13, 71; witches and 43–5; Woman idea and 82–4, 102–4; women in Bible and 37–8
Piaf, E. 96
Plato 23
politics, psychoanalysis and 21–9
Pontalis, J. B. 58
pop music, melancholic feminine of 96–9
Possession (film) 59, 72
Powers of horror: An essay on abjection (Kristeva) 23–4
Pretty Little Liars (TV show) 107
Prometheus (film) 57

psychiatry, neoliberal capitalism and 113–5
psychoanalysis: Imaginary and 12–3; Lacanian (*see* Lacanian psychoanalysis); monstrous mother and 67–8; mother-monster and (*see* mother-monster, psychoanalysis and); Other relationship and 11, 70–1; politics and 21–9; Real and 12, 13–4, 27–8; sexual difference and 1–2; Symbolic and 12–3; woman in 66–72
Psy-complex 114, 118

Ragland-Sullivan, E. 16
Real, Lacanian psychoanalysis and 12, 13–4, 27–8
reconciliation 93
Reddit 73
Return America 128
Riggs, D. W. 103
Ring, The (film) 72
Rivers, D. J. 127
Roe v. Wade 1
Rose, J. 81
Rosemary's Baby (film) 59
Ross, A. S. 127
Ruti, M. 21

saints: feminine jouissance and 39–42; mythology and 39–45
Saint Teresa of Ávila 39–40
Sansome, L. A. 112
Sansome, R. A. 112
Schwartz-Salant, N. 117–8
Scott, R. 57
self-harming behavior 116–7
sexual difference: film use in study of 6–9; horror and 2, 3–6; introduction to 1–3; Lacanian psychoanalysis and 1–2; medical gaze and (*see* medical gaze, sexual difference and); in mythology (*see* mythology, sexual difference in); the Other relationship and 1–2; psychoanalytic conspiracy theory about 73–4; transgender people and (*see* transgender people)
sexuation: abjection, Kristeva and 22–4; becoming-woman and 10–29; Deleuze and Guattari's philosophy 24–6; Imaginary and 12–3; jouissance and 14–5; Lacanian psychoanalysis of 15–21; Lacanian subject 11–2; molar identity of woman and 26–9; object a and 15; overview of 10–1; politics, psychoanalysis and 21–9; Real and 12, 13–4; Symbolic and 12–3; tripartite positions of 15–6; Zupančič notion of 18
Simone, N. 96
Sirens, as monstrous-feminine 33–4
Skott-Myhre, H. 114, 119, 121
Skott-Myhre, K. 42, 77, 86
Smith, M. 43, 44
Smith, S. 77, 78, 79–80, 83
"Snow White" (Brothers Grimm) 91; Evil Queen as femme fatale 91–6
Snow White and the Huntsman (film) 92, 93, 94
Snow White and the Seven Dwarfs (film) 92
Sobchak, V. 89
Soler, C. 14, 16, 19, 65, 80, 90, 97, 98, 103–4
Spears, B. 97
Sperber, E. 132
Sprenger, J. 44–5
Stern, A. 112
Stevens, A. 17
Studler, G. 106
Sugarman, J. 113–4
Sullivan, N. 131–2
Swales, S. 21, 127
Symbolic: gender politics and 13; Kristeva and 23; Lacanian psychoanalysis and 12–3; sexual difference and 13

10 Things I Hate About You (film) 96
Theron, C. 92
Thousand Plateaus, A (Deleuze and Guattari) 24, 84
Toft, M. 54–5, 62
transgender people 124–34; bathrooms and 127–31; becoming 131–3; Lacanian perspectives on 124–6; memes, use of 127–9; overview of 124; *vs.* transsexual label 125
transgenerational transmission of trauma (TTT) 56
transmogrification 131
trauma 58
Turner, V. 119

unconscious, mother-monster of 67–72
Under the Skin (film) 99
Urban Legend (film) 91
U'Ren, R. 114–5
USA Today 124

Vanier, A. 12, 13
Verhaghe, P. 125
Von Trier, L. 75

Warring-Curran, J. 53–4
Williams, L. 5
Winehouse, A. 97
Witch, The (film) 73
witches: feminine jouissance and 42–5; mythology and 39–45; word origin 42

Woman: Lacan notion of 3, 16–7, 19; as Other 58–9; as partial objects 60–1; in psychoanalysis 66–72
woman-mother, deterritorializing 82–4
women: in Bible 36–9; with BPD 120–1; maternal imagination/impressions and 52–4; who has it all 99–104; as witches 43–4
Wood, R. 57
Woolf, V. 27, 47

Yates, A. 77, 78–80, 83

Zevnik, A. 29
Zizek, S. 21, 95
Zupančič, A. 18, 27, 28, 29